CW00417344

40 Coast and
Country Walks

The author and publisher have made every effort to ensure that the information in this publication is accurate, and accept no responsibility whatsoever for any loss, injury or inconvenience experienced by any person or persons whilst using this book.

published by
pocket mountains ltd
The Old Church, Annanside, Moffat, DG10 9HB
pocketmountains.com

ISBN: 978-1-907025-52-5

Text © 2016 John Fergusson. Photography © 2016 John Fergusson
except p66 © Fraser Dixon and pp7, 20 and 30 © Fionn McArthur

A catalogue record for this book is available from the British Library

Contains Ordnance Survey data © Crown copyright and database right 2016, supported by out of copyright mapping 1945-1961

Printed in Poland

Introduction

If you are reading this book because you have decided to explore Orkney on foot, then well done! There is no better place to lace up the boots and set off across sandy beaches, beside stunning cliffs, up coastal paths or along quiet country roads. Interest lies around every corner; history and wildlife so close you can touch them and there is so much archaeology you are almost in danger of tripping over it. In recent years cafés, craft shops, hostels and heritage centres have been establishing themselves on most of the islands, and the network of buses, ferries and planes make them remarkably easy to get to. For residents and visitors alike, especially those who love the great outdoors, Orkney is a wonderful place to be.

History

Orkney's history is longer than most. Archaeologists have evidence of human activity dating back 9000 years, from soon after the last ice age. Since the first arrival of nomadic hunters, humans have left their mark. Neolithic houses, Iron Age brochs, Pictish artwork, Viking churches, and medieval castles and palaces, right through to 20th-century fortifications, history is everywhere and very tangible. Outwith the most famous sites, visitors are free to wander through, round and among standing stones, burial tombs and gun emplacements. Access is usually unsupervised, and visitors can linger and ponder as long as they like. There are

superb museums in Kirkwall, Stromness and Lyness, not forgetting the farm museums at Corrigall and Kirbister, and a network of local and island heritage centres. They make an excellent job of bringing Orkney's long story to life.

Walking in Orkney

Orkney is famous for its changeable weather and the old line about 'four seasons in one day' is a joke, but only just. Check the local weather forecast before you go and be prepared, regardless of the season. Good footwear is a must and it is always sensible to carry a waterproof jacket and trousers, even if the day starts off sunny. Several of the routes in this guide follow cliff edges and great care should be taken, particularly when walking with children. On some of the smaller islands it is not possible to buy food, yet the ferry times may require you to spend several hours there, so be sure to take a flask and something to eat. Elsewhere, Orkney's rural and island shops struggle valiantly to provide a local service and it is good to support them where you can. Mobile phone reception in Orkney is surprisingly good, but do not rely on getting a signal when you need it. Always make sure someone knows where you are going and when you expect to return.

Access

Scotland's liberal access laws, allowing the public freedom to roam the countryside regardless of whether it is privately owned or not, are enshrined in the Land Reform (Scotland) Act 2003. These rights are balanced by responsibilities to treat the land, and those who make their living from it, with respect and consideration. Leave gates as you find them, try not to climb fences, avoid walking through crops and always take your litter home.

Dogs and birdlife

There are certain times of year – during lambing, calving or the bird-nesting seasons – when a rampaging labrador can do great harm. Dogs should always be kept under proper control – and on a lead near livestock. Groundnesting birds have enough trouble coping with nature's predators without having to contend with family pets as well. Seal pups could be abandoned if your dog separates them from their mother. Do not enter a field where there are cattle with calves at foot. It should go without saying to clean up after your pet. Sadly, many people don't bother. Please don't be one of them.

Orkney is brilliant for birdwatching, but there are some birds you need to watch closer than others. The great skua, aka the bonxie, is the bull-terrier of the bird world. Get too close to its nest or its young and it will not hesitate to attack to drive you away. Likewise the Arctic tern, sleek and sporty, can scare the living daylights out of anyone who strays too close to its colony in the breeding season. Generally speaking, from late April until the

beginning of August it is important to avoid disruption to the nesting sites by sticking to established paths where they exist and backing off if you see signs of visibly agitated birds, alarm calling and mock (or actual!) dive bombing. If you do find yourself under attack, hold a stick or jacket above your head and clear the area as quickly as possible. To get the most from your visit, it is worth equipping yourself with a good bird book. Those produced in the islands also tend to include the local names, helping you to tell a Sula (Gannet) from a Scarf (Cormorant), and a Loon (Red-Throated Diver) from Little Footy-Arse (it's a Grebe. Honestly!)

Travel

Buses in Orkney operate on a 'hail and ride' principle, meaning you can ask the driver to pick you up or drop you off wherever you want – as long as it is on the route. A number of the North and South Isles have local buses which meet ferries, although several only run a part-time service and must be pre-booked. Check ferry times carefully as some routes must be booked in advance and some crossings are 'on request'. That means the ferry might not sail if you have not told them you will be waiting. Flights to the North Isles of Orkney run frequently, but seats are in great demand. Book as far in advance as possible for the best chance of a ticket. The tourist information centre in Kirkwall should be able to provide timetables and booking information.

About this guide

The 40 walks in this guide range from a short stroll to hikes of several hours, but most can be completed in half a day or less. The majority are circular, several are lollipop-shaped and some require you to return by the same route. They all, however, end up back where they started, so you will not find yourself miles from your car. Each route is prefaced by an indication of the distance involved and the time it is likely to take. The latter is estimated on the time it took the author to walk the route (averaging around 3.5km per hour) before adding a little for tea, toilet and tourism stops. The timings should be regarded as a rough guide, and if you have to catch a bus or boat at the end of the walk, leave plenty of extra time! Only on a couple of routes will you be asked to set off across the heather without a path to follow, and never without your immediate destination being in view in clear visibility. That said, walking in Orkney should not be underestimated and good visibility cannot be relied upon. The sketch maps are to help in planning your trip and are not sufficiently detailed to navigate by. It is advisable to carry the relevant Ordnance Survey map. Any compass directions are approximate, and lefts and rights are relative to the direction of travel. Where a walk involves crossing to a tidal island, it will be mentioned in the notes. Always ensure you get reliable advice on the state of the tides before crossing. If you get it wrong, you could have a cold, wet and lonely few hours before getting back across.

Pronunciation advice

Visitors will be met throughout Orkney with goodwill, but you can earn extra Brownie points by avoiding some common mistakes. 1. Orkney should never be referred to as 'The Orkneys'. It is Orkney or, if you want to be very formal, The Orkney Islands. 2. The biggest island in Orkney is called 'the Mainland', not 'Mainland'. It requires the definite article at all times. 3. Islands and parishes ending in 'ay' – that is most of them – have no emphasis on the final syllable (e.g. Westray rhymes with 'vestry', Sanday with 'brandy' and Harray with 'marry'). North Ronaldsay, Rousay, Birsay etc all follow the same rule. The same applies to most places names: Stromness, Deerness and Tankerness are pronounced like 'fondness' with the 'ness' being almost dropped. Among the exceptions is Finstown which prefers equal emphasis across both syllables. Likewise, Orphir is simply 'Or-fur', and never 'Or-fear'.

Particular places mentioned in this guide which require careful pronunciation include Egilsay (AY-gillsay), Noltland (NOWT-lan), Brodgar (BROD-yer), Brough should rhyme with 'loch', Quoy sounds like the 'River Kwai' (e.g. Kwai-loo), Doun Helzie is pronounced 'Doon Helly' and Wideford is 'WIDE-fud', never 'Widdy-ford'. The parish of Holm is pronounced 'ham'. Islands with holm in their name (e.g. Lamb Holm) are pronounced 'home', and Rothiesholm in Stronsay is pronounced 'Rouse-um'.

'Best kens' as an Orcadian might say – roughly translated as 'Go figure!'

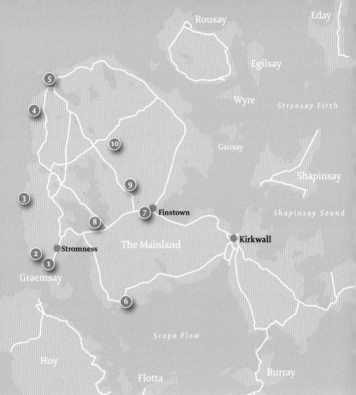

The West Mainland includes the Heart of Neolithic Orkney, the four ancient monuments which were collectively given World Heritage Site status by UNESCO in 1999. Maeshowe, Skara Brae, The Ring of Brodgar and The Standing Stones of Stenness are just the flagships of one of the richest surviving Neolithic landscapes in Europe – there are many more fascinating sites to explore!

Stromness, the West Mainland's principal centre of population, sits on the shores of Hamnavoe – Old Norse for Haven Bay. It is a town shaped by history and the sea, with narrow winding streets, curiously named alleyways and a busy harbour. Apart from its role as one of Orkney's main ferry ports it is also the centre of the local diving industry, taking divers out to explore the wrecks of the German Fleet scuttled in Scapa Flow in 1919.

The Ring of Brodgar ▶

The West Mainland

Brinkie's Brae and Stromness

Distance 7km **Time** 2 hours 30
Terrain steep lanes and paths initially,
boggy moorland, then minor roads and
tracks **Map** OS Explorer 463 **Access** bus
from Kirkwall to Stromness

With its narrow winding streets, stone
piers and steep lanes, the port of
Stromness has a unique charm. There is
no better place from which to enjoy the
town and the bustling activity on the
water than from the granite ridge of
Brinkie's Brae that overlooks it.

Parking is free on Ferry Road, between
the Co-op supermarket and the ferry
terminal. Set off with the water on your
left. At the Stromness Hotel, head left
into Victoria Street until you reach Boy's
Lane on the right immediately before the
Royal Hotel. This steep and narrow alley
brings you out on Franklin Road in front

of the Old Stromness Academy, now a
business centre.

Turn right, past the old school steps,
and take the lane at the end of the wall
which continues up to the public road.
Cross into Downie's Lane and
immediately take the steps up the bank
on your left-hand side. Ignore the path by
the drystane dyke, but take the steps
which appear on your right and climb up
the steep hillside to a stone bench set
into a wall. This is a good place to take a
breather and the view provides a great
excuse. When ready, continue uphill,
turning right along the granite dyke to
the trig point. The hard work is over!

Head left, following the line of the fence
across the heather. It can be quite wet
underfoot. Halfway down, the path runs
along a tumbledown dyke between two
fences and emerges onto a quiet road.

Brunt Hill

Stromness Reservoir

waterworks

The Loons

Mewie Hill

Stromness

Brinkies Brae

Brownstown Road

Old Academy

A965

Hannavoe

Inner Holm

Outer Holm

Point of Ness

0   1km

Turn left and follow the road as it bends round to the right, until you are walking along the other side of the valley. The area of marshy ground to your right is known as 'The Loons'.

At the Stromness Water Treatment Works sign, take the road to your left and head uphill to the reservoir. Walk up the steps of the dam and go right along the wall before turning left to follow the path around the water. When you arrive back at the dam, turn right up the track. At the brow, where the track goes through a field gate, branch left along the edge of the heather moorland to the corner where you will find a track dropping down the slope between fields.

Turn left at the junction onto what soon becomes a surfaced road, following it until it bends left between two houses. Continue straight ahead up the short track, which becomes a rough footpath running down past some old farm buildings. Turn right onto Brownstown Road to walk down the hill.

Head left at the crossroads and, a short distance later, go straight across the mini-roundabout, taking care at this sometimes busy junction. After 100m, where the main road swings up to the right, branch downhill into Hellihole Road. Walk past the two navigational markers – used to guide shipping through the harbour channel – until you find yourself at the bottom of the hill.

This is the main street of Stromness which goes by several names as it meanders through town, 'uncoiled like a sailor's rope from North to South', according to the Orcadian poet George Mackay Brown. Turn left and follow it through the town to the Stromness Hotel.

◀ Stromness with Brinkie's Brae behind

The Ness to Breckness

Distance 9km **Time** 3 hours
Terrain coastal paths, beaches and minor roads **Map** OS Explorer 463
Access bus from Kirkwall to Stromness

Warebeth Beach has long been a place of work and play for the people of Stromness. Washed by the Atlantic swell, it sits on the western approaches to Scapa Flow, looking over to the cliffs of Hoy. A lively walk on a windy day!

If you are coming by car, drive through Stromness to the Point of Ness Caravan & Camping Site and park when you can drive no further. The path sets off to your right, beside the golf course, so beware of wind-assisted golf balls which overshoot the 16th green.

The old military buildings, set into the banks beside the path, are reminders of Scapa Flow's importance in wartime. The Ness Battery, which you will soon see on your right, has a well-preserved accommodation block. Tours are offered over the summer months, but must be booked in advance.

Continue along the path to the cemetery, passing the few rusting remains of a Norwegian fishing boat which ran aground in 1966. Follow the path along the outside of the cemetery wall to the beach at Warebeth, known for its fish fossils. In the 18th and 19th centuries, kelp was harvested here, dried, then burned in pits for its potash content.

Take the farm track above the beach, and branch left along the shoreline when the track turns inland. The footpath soon narrows and becomes uneven and, at times, it is easier to walk along the shore.

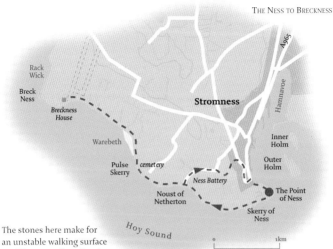

The stones here make for an unstable walking surface – ankles are easily twisted – so proceed with care.

When you arrive below the ruined buildings, head up through the wire gate, with an electric fence immediately behind it. The gate is of a type commonly found across Orkney, comprising several strands of wire, supported by poles and pulled tight across the opening. They are opened by loosening the catch at one end, relaxing the wires while you step through, then securing it tightly again. To pass through the electric fence, unhook the insulated handle and replace it carefully behind you.

Breckness is privately owned so there may be livestock around the buildings. The most ruinous is the 17th-century Breckness House, built for the last Bishop of Orkney, which hints at former grandeur with impressive fireplaces and carved stones still visible.

When you are ready, return along the shore to the cemetery. Some 500m further on, take the surfaced road which leads inland and winds gently uphill past the speed limit signs. Just after the road bends left, take the track on the right to head between a wall and a fence. Ness Camp is across the field to your right.

Where the track meets a wall, go left and walk up to the Gun Viewpoint, with a fine view out over the golf course and Hoy Sound. From there, take the path that heads north towards the wooden houses, following it downhill to join Back Road, with wooden houses first on your right-hand side, then on your left. Turn right at the junction with Back Road to walk downhill to the seafront. The Ness campsite is a short distance to your right with the parking area just beyond.

◀ Old croft at Breckness

Yesnaby and the Castles

Distance 8km (out and back)
Time 3 hours **Terrain** high coastal path
Map OS Explorer 463 **Access** no public
transport to the start

Enjoy one of the most impressive
stretches of cliff on Orkney's west coast
with two – nearly three – magnificent
rock stacks. The walk offers a glimpse of
the Old Man of Hoy in the distance and
the prospect of a close encounter with
primula scotica, the rare Scottish primrose.

The walk starts from the wartime
buildings at the end of Orkney's Yesnaby road,
signposted from the B9056. This was a
practice range for Second World War
gunners who fired at targets towed behind
aircraft offshore. Spare a thought for the
pilots of those aircraft as you park your car.

Information boards help to explain the
spectacular rock formations of the
coastline. They may tempt you to delay
your start to seek out the fossilised sand
ripples and mud cracks nearby.

With the sea to your right, head down
the slope towards the stone fencepost. To
your left is prime *primula scotica* territory,
and one of the best places to find this tiny
and endangered plant. It flowers in May
and July. Look for a distinctive purple
flower with five heart-shaped petals.

At the bottom of the slope the path
crosses a footbridge and wooden steps
before turning right. Ahead is a short
detour onto a promontory called the
Brough of Bigging, from where the
Old Man of Hoy is often visible against
the cliffs 16km to the south. When leaving

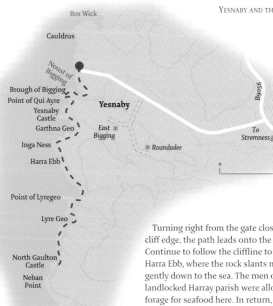

Bor Wick

Cauldrus

Noust of Bigging

Brough of Bigging
Point of Qui Ayre
Yesnaby Castle
Garthna Geo

Inga Ness

Harra Ebb

Point of Lyregeo

Lyre Geo

North Gaulton Castle
Neban Point

Bight of Mousland

Yesnaby

East Bigging

Roundadee

To Stromness

B9056

0   1km

Turning right from the gate close to the cliff edge, the path leads onto the heath. Continue to follow the cliffline to the Harra Ebb, where the rock slants more gently down to the sea. The men of landlocked Harray parish were allowed to forage for seafood here. In return, Sandwick men could take peat from the Harray hills.

The path continues to wind its way south, round the Geo of Inganess, over a burn and past Lyre Geo. Then, as you walk over the shoulder of the hill, you will see your destination. North Gaulton Castle is the only sea stack in Orkney (or, most probably, anywhere) to have been used as a car park. In 1994, a helicopter lowered a Rover saloon onto the stack for an advertising campaign.

It is possible to continue along the coast for another 10km to Stromness but, as your car is parked at Yesnaby, this is a good point to begin retracing your steps to the start.

the Brough, turn right and follow the path across rocks thrown up by the winter storms. This area was once used for quarrying millstones and an abandoned project can be seen in the turf by the fence.

Soon the path passes close to two rock stacks. The first, the Castle of Qui Ayre, remains tenuously attached to the cliff by a single slab of rock, so it is technically an arch. A short distance beyond, there can be no doubting Yesnaby Castle's claim to sea stack status. Those who come to conquer it must be able to swim as well as climb.

Marwick Head

Distance 5.5km **Time** 2 hours
Terrain high coastal cliff path, returning
on minor roads **Map** OS Explorer 463
Access no public transport to the start

Best avoided by those without a head
for heights, this path leads to some of
the most spectacular cliffs in Orkney
and a memorial to Lord Kitchener
(the iconic mustachioed face of First
World War recruitment posters) and the
crew of *HMS Hampshire*.

Park at Marwick, which is well
signposted off the B9056 roughly halfway
between Birsay and Skaill. If the tide is
out, there is a lot to explore on the beach
and in the rockpools. The ebbing tide
leaves behind a lagoon, called the Choin,
which attracts a variety of ducks and

waders. The boiler of the steamship
Monomoy, wrecked in 1896, is still visible
below the car park.

Before heading north to the cliffs, turn
left and follow the track south for 700m to
Sand Geo. Local fishermen built the huts
here after the *Monomoy* came ashore in
their usual landing place at Marwick.
The winch, which once hauled fishing
boats up from the shore, is said to have
come from the wreck.

When you are ready to tackle the
cliffs, retrace your steps past the car park
and continue onto the path behind the
beach. The drystane dyke, supported by
buttresses, makes a great place for some

concealed birdwatching. All sorts of gulls feed on the beach, along with turnstone and redshank, with eider duck out on the water and shelduck in summer.

Once you reach the end of the wall, the path continues round the shore before turning uphill. As the cliffs get higher, the climb gets steeper. In summer the area is a colourful carpet of sea pinks and sea campion, bird's-foot trefoil and kidney vetch. Soon the Kitchener Memorial, visible from the car park but then hidden by the cliffs, starts to reappear over the brow of the hill and the scale of the cliffs of Marwick Head can be appreciated.

In a good season, there can be as many as 25,000 seabirds on the cliffs at Marwick Head, according to the RSPB. The birds are probably best viewed from the point at which you first see the full 100m face. A stone, set on its end close to the cliff, provides a safe vantage point for anyone without a head for heights. From here, as you approach the Kitchener Memorial, the cliffs drop out of sight.

The memorial tower was erected in 1926,

paid for by public subscription, to honour Lord Kitchener, Secretary of State for War, who was lost when *HMS Hampshire* sank after apparently striking a mine off Marwick Head in 1916. A more recent memorial wall has been added to commemorate the many other men who lost their lives on board.

After continuing along the clifftop for 400m, the path heads right, through a kissing gate and down between fields to a parking area by Mid Comloquoy. Turn right along the minor road and right again at the junction to walk downhill to the sea. The buttressed wall is to your left and, beyond it, you can see the car park at the far end of the bay.

◀ The Kitchener Memorial on Marwick Head

15

The Brough of Birsay and Skiba Geo

Distance **5km** Time **2 hours**
Terrain **tidal causeway and grass
footpaths** Map **OS Explorer 463**
Access **only possible for two hours either
side of low tide. Check the tide times
with the tourist information centre or
ask locally. Buses run to the village in
Birsay, a 15-minute walk from the start**

**Cross a tidal causeway to the place the
Vikings called Fortress Island, with
ancient monuments and seabird
colonies, before heading along the
coastal path to the fisherman's hut at
Skiba Geo.**

The stretch of water which separates the
Brough from the mainland makes this an
exciting place to visit – provided you get
the timing right. More than a few
unsuspecting visitors have found
their return blocked by the in-rushing
tide, and their stay forcibly extended
by eight hours.

If you arrived by bus, head out of the
village, known as The Palace, and follow
the road past the ruins of the 16th-century
residence of the unpopular Robert Stewart,
Earl of Orkney. The road continues round
the shore to the car park on the headland.

The concrete causeway, easily seen from
the car park at low tide, winds its way
across the rocks. Once on the far side, you
can either visit the remains of the old
Norse settlement, where a fee is payable to
Historic Scotland in the summer months,
or head straight onto the hillside. The
structural remains here show evidence of
Christian, Pictish and Viking occupation,
but it was the Vikings who gave the island
its name: Birsay is a derivation of *Byrgisey*,
Norse for 'Fortress Island'.

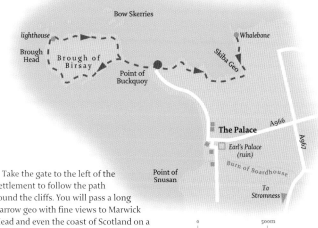

Take the gate to the left of the settlement to follow the path round the cliffs. You will pass a long narrow geo with fine views to Marwick Head and even the coast of Scotland on a clear day. The path climbs gradually to the western headland and along to the lighthouse. It was built by David Alan Stevenson in 1925. He was also responsible for the lighthouse at Noup Head in Westray, which can be seen 26km to the northeast in clear weather.

The cliffs below the lighthouse are often busy with seabirds. In the early summer guillemot, razorbill, fulmar and even puffin nest along this stretch, and there are several good places to watch the activity. From here the path continues round the north end of the island until it brings you back to the causeway. Once back on the mainland, head left from the car park along the top of the low cliffs.

Keep an eye open for seals as you make your way to Skiba Geo (also called Skippi

Geo), the sheltered bay used by local fishermen over the centuries. The recesses by the stone hut, set out like splayed segments of an orange, are boat nousts, used for storing boats out of the wind.

Steep stone steps lead down to the beach. Walk beyond Skiba Geo to the next headland. The jaw of a whale was put here towards the end of the 19th century, perhaps as a fisherman's marker, and has been in this spot ever since. It is known simply as The Whalebone.

When you have soaked up the scenery and the atmosphere, return to your car (or bus) and, if you have time, visit the Birsay Bay Tearoom on the far side of the village. They are justly proud of their baking and home-grown fruit and vegetables.

◀ The Whalebone at Birsay

The Earl's Bu and Orphir Bay

Distance 3.5km **Time** 1 hour 30
Terrain grassy paths and minor roads
Map OS Explorer 463 **Access** buses from
Kirkwall to Houton – ask the driver to
drop you at the Gyre road end, 800m from
the start

If you want to know more about the
Viking Earls who ruled Orkney a
thousand years ago, this is a good place
to start. There is a lot to learn from the
delightful Orkneyinga Saga Centre before
heading along the shores of Scapa Flow.

The exhibition and video in the little
building by the car park at the Earl's Bu
and Church (signposted from the A964
between Orphir village and the Houton
ferry terminal) tell the story of the Viking
Earls and their enduring influence on
Orkney. Although unstaffed, it is anything
but a stuffy history lesson.

On the path to the kirkyard, you will
pass the low foundations of a complex
of old buildings, thought to be part of
the 12th-century Earl's Bu (manor house)
mentioned in the Viking Sagas. Pass
through the gates to visit what's left of
the only remaining circular medieval
church in Scotland. It is said to have been
built by Earl Hakon, infamous for
ordering the execution of his pious
cousin and co-ruler Magnus – or St
Magnus as he was later to become. To do
penance Hakon went on a pilgrimage to
Jerusalem and modelled the church on
similar structures seen on his travels in
the Holy Land. It remained intact until
around 1750 when its stones were used to
build a new church, since demolished.

Leave the churchyard by the gate in the
left-hand wall and walk down to the
shore, turning left over a footbridge and

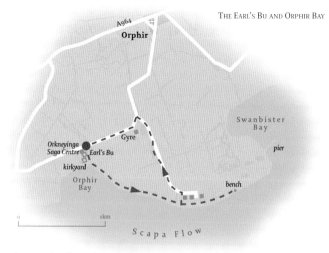

onto the coastal path. For the next 1km, you will be walking alongside a drystane dyke, covered with brittle, bushy lichen – a sure sign of clean air.

Wildflowers add colour to the low-lying cliffs in summer. Look for the yellow kidney vetch and the purple devil's bit scabious standing out among the creeping willow, heather and crowberry.

When the dyke ends, continue above the shore, past a low marker post and a pair of stone fishermen's huts, to the bench facing out to sea on the headland. It looks over the stretch of water where Squadron Commander Edwin Dunning changed the face of naval warfare in August 1917 when he became the first person to land an aircraft successfully on the deck of a moving ship. Unfortunately he was killed a few days later trying to do it again.

Retrace your steps past the stone huts until you reach the marker post. Turn right and follow the fence inland to a small parking area, now turning left along the public road. The road descends gradually before climbing again, now flanked by gorse and – unusually for Orkney – trees.

Look for the sign on the left directing you to the woodland path through a small area of sycamore, ash, rowan and wych elm. It provides a haven for woodland birds and insects and, being downstream from the old millpond, is also frequented by otters.

Back on the road, ignore the track leading left to Gyre house and farm; instead walk another 230m to the junction, where a left turn will lead you back to the Orkneyinga Saga Centre. If you want to catch a bus back to Kirkwall, a right turn at the junction will lead to Orphir village, 1.3km along the road.

Binscarth Woods and Wasdale

Distance 5km (there and back)
Time 2 hours **Terrain** fields, farm tracks
and muddy paths **Map** OS Explorer 463
Access buses from Kirkwall and
Stromness to Finstown

**A rare opportunity in Orkney to walk
through mature woodland which should
not be missed. The old drover's road
leads through the trees and over the
hillside to Wasdale Loch.**

There are parking bays at the side of the
A965 opposite the Finstown village shop.
An Irish veteran of the Napoleonic Wars
called David Phin opened an alehouse
called the Toddy Hole here in 1820 and the
village has been known as 'Phin's Toon'
ever since. The road through the village is
busy, but you only need follow it up the
hill for 100m before passing through a
kissing gate on the right. This takes you
onto a grass track across the field and
down to a gate into Binscarth Woods.

While the mature woodland ahead dates
from the 19th century, the plantation to
the right was planted in 1990. The 18
different species appear to be doing well,
disproving the myth that trees cannot
thrive in Orkney.

Once through the gate and over the
stone bridge, there is a choice of routes.
For an easy, straightforward walk
continue up the old road until it emerges
onto the drive to Binscarth House.
Alternatively, go through the gate in the
wall to your left and follow the path along
the side of the burn. You will need to
clamber across at least one fallen tree and,
at times, the path will be muddy. The
woods are popular with rooks and in the
spring, when the woodland is carpeted
with bluebells, it can be a noisy place.

If you took the path along the burn, it
will eventually turn right to rejoin the old
road by the gate onto the drive to
Binscarth House.

From here, go through the gate and
walk up the track for 150m until it bends

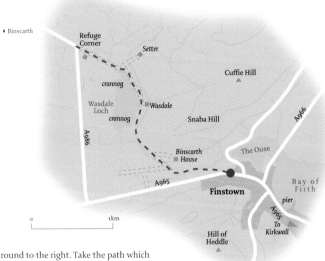

◀ Binscarth

Refuge Corner

Setter

Cuffie Hill

crannog

Wasdale Loch

Wasdale

crannog

Snaba Hill

A986

Binscarth House

The Ouse

A965

Finstown

Bay of Firth

pier

A965
To Kirkwall

A966

0   1km

Hill of Heddle

round to the right. Take the path which continues straight ahead between bushes and drystane dykes. Through a break in the gorse, look for Howe Harper, the burial chamber on the hillside just above you. There is said to be a curse on anyone who excavates it!

Go through a gate and down towards Wasdale Loch. The little island is a crannog – an ancient man-made dwelling built on the water – and the stones are all that remain of what is believed to have been a chapel.

The path continues between the fields until it joins the farm track, then it hugs the shoreline round to the north end of the loch. It's a great place for birdwatching and you might even be lucky enough to spot an otter. There is

another crannog at this end of the loch which is gradually being subsumed into the shoreline.

As the track heads west towards the main road and the end of the walk, wetlands to your left again offer the promise of interesting wildlife.

The gravel track joins the main road at a bend known as the Refuge Corner, named, so local lore has it, because a tenant evicted from his home lived in the field for many years in a shelter made out of his old box bed.

From here you can either hail a bus back to Finstown, or retrace your steps to the starting point, perhaps taking the other route through the woods.

Around the Ness of Brodgar

Distance 6km **Time** 2 hours 30
Terrain flat grassy paths and a short
stretch of public road **Map** OS Explorer 463
Access bus from Kirkwall and Stromness
passes within 700m of the stones – ask
the driver to stop at the Brodgar road

**The strip of land between the Harray and
Stenness Lochs holds a vast expanse of
prehistoric buildings below the ground,
as well as the famous stones which stand
above it. Enjoy this peaceful stroll around
the Ness of Brodgar, in the Heart of
Neolithic Orkney.**

The walk starts from the public car park
on the B9055, around 350m from the Ring
of Brodgar, close to the Harray Loch.
Take the boardwalk to the public road, crossing
carefully – it's not busy but traffic can be
travelling quite fast – and go through the
gate onto the wide path up to the Ring
of Brodgar.

This iconic stone circle was erected
sometime between 2500BC and 2000BC.

Outside the massive ditch which
surrounds it (and which, incredibly, was
used for tank driving practice in the
Second World War) is a landscape rich in
archaeology. After a turn around the stone
circle, and with your back to the road, take
the path across the grass to Salt Knowe,
an earth mound which looks like a burial
chamber. In fact, it is just a mound of
earth with no structure hidden within.

Whatever the original purpose, at
almost 6m above the surrounding land it
is a good spot to spy archaeological
points of interest nearby. Continue down
to the Stenness Loch, turning left at the
water's edge. This loch is brackish, with
varying levels of salt content, allowing it
to support a wide range of wildlife suited
to both salt and freshwater conditions.

The path follows the side of the loch,
turning left just before Brodgar Farm, the
first buildings you encounter, to join the
public road. Cross the road – again be wary
of speeding motorists – and drop onto the

◀ Standing Stones of Stenness

footpath on the other side, turning right along the side of the Harray Loch.

Between the lochs, the land to your right is where recent archaeological excavations have revealed an extensive and exciting complex of Neolithic buildings. In size and sophistication, it's up there with Stonehenge or the Great Pyramids of ancient Egypt. It predates both, however, as the site was possibly occupied from 3500BC up to the end of the Neolithic period 1500 years later, when it was mysteriously abandoned – then forgotten about for another 4000 years.

Where the footpath ends, step back onto the public road to cross the causeway. Ahead is a huge monolith called the Watchstone, the sole survivor of a pair of standing stones which once stood either side of the causeway. The entrance to the enclosure around the Standing Stones of Stenness is 100m

along the road. These huge megaliths – the tallest is 6m high – are all that remain of an ancient ring believed to date from around 3100BC, making it one of the oldest henge sites in the British Isles.

Leave by the stile in the corner opposite the entrance. This is close to the site of the Odin Stone, where local couples used to plight their troth while holding hands through a hole in the centre. Sadly, it was destroyed in 1814 by the local farmer, Captain MacKay, who was fed up with people coming onto his land.

Cross the stile and turn right along the path to the Barnhouse Settlement, a village dating from around the same time as the Standing Stones of Stenness.

Retrace your steps along the path, but ignore the stile and walk back to the road. Turn right to cross back over the causeway and follow the footpath beside the road back to the Ring of Brodgar.

The Knowes of Trotty

Distance 4km **Time** 1 hour 30 (there and back) **Terrain** moorland path through sometimes dense heather; boggy in places **Map** OS Explorer 463 **Access** buses to Dounby pass within 600m of the start – ask the driver to drop you at Grimeston Road, then head up Howe Road opposite

A short walk to one of Orkney's most important – and peaceful – archaeological sites. Almost worth going for the name alone.

The start is on the minor road which branches northeast off the A986 at the sign to Howe. There is a small parking area on the right-hand side, 600m from the A-road, where the minor road turns sharp left. Walk up the farm track until you pass the house and steading of Winksetter on your right.

Follow the track as it bends round the end of the fence to the left. After 100m, where the track goes right, step onto the old peat road which continues close to the fence. After it dives into the heather, it can be difficult to see where the path goes at times, but keep heading roughly towards the fields on the far hill and you will not get lost. Boardwalks will keep you on the right track and help you over the wettest bits.

The air is usually filled with birdsong. Alongside the ever-present curlew and greylag geese, listen out for skylark in spring and autumn, and keep an eye open for hen harrier hunting over the heather.

It is only when you reach the first of the knowes, and stand on its summit, that you can begin to appreciate how special this site is. Beside you, running north to

south, are two lines of burial mounds, not all easy to spot. Once there were around 20 mounds, but erosion – not least by rabbits – has reduced their number to the 12 which can be seen today.

This is the largest Bronze Age burial site in Scotland and dates from the days when the dead started to be buried in individual graves, rather than interred in communal tombs. A 19th-century excavation of the largest of the mounds turned up four paper-thin decorated gold discs which are believed to have covered conical buttons. The gold is of Scottish origin, but the discs are similar to others found in Ireland and southern England suggesting that, even in 2000BC, people living in this part of the world were either well-connected or well-travelled.

You are unlikely to be disturbed during your visit and, without being disrespectful

to the dead, it is a fine place to enjoy a picnic on top of the knowe of your choice, before returning through the heather to Winksetter Farm and down the road to your car.

And the name? Trotty translates from Old Norse as 'Trow Marsh'. Trows were goblin-like creatures of legend who only came out at night and were bent on causing mischief. So the Knowes of Trotty means something along the lines of 'The Mounds beside the Marshes where the Goblins Live'.

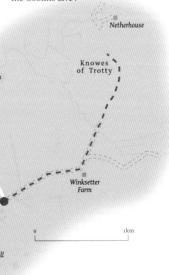

Netherhouse

Knowes of Trotty

Geroin

Howe Road

Howe Farm

To Dounby

Bimbister

A986

Winksetter Farm

To Finstown and Kirkwall

To Grimeston

0   1km

Kame of Corrigall

Distance 8.5km **Time** 2 hours 30
Terrain boggy peat roads and deep
heather moorland, with minor roads to
finish **Map** OS Explorer 463 **Access** buses
to Dounby, 2.5km from the start

Old peat roads through the Harray hills
lead to the top of the Kame of Corrigall
where the view more than compensates
for the effort invested. Orkney's great
natural amphitheatre – the Heart of
Neolithic Orkney – is all laid out before
you. Superb!

From the crossroads in Dounby, take the
B9057 (signposted to Evie), but turn right
after 1.7km onto a track towards the wind
turbine. Park on the hard standing at the
top of the track, making sure you don't
hinder access. An old peat road, unused
for many years, takes up where the gravel
track leaves off.

With the wind turbine to your right,
follow the old road – now little more
than a mossy depression in the heather –
as it sets off into the moorland. Soon
it will curve gently right to head through
the heather into the wide valley.
Stay on the old road or beside it if the
walking is easier, keeping right if in
doubt at any forks, as you walk along
the contour line.

This old road was used by generations
of local families to bring peat down from
the hills. It may have been cheap and
plentiful, but peat required a huge effort
to harvest. The Corrigall Farm Museum,
which sits under the other side of the hill,
is a great place to learn about rural life
and peat cutting in days gone by.

Eventually the old road bends round to
the right and starts to climb for a distance
of about 250m, ending where it meets

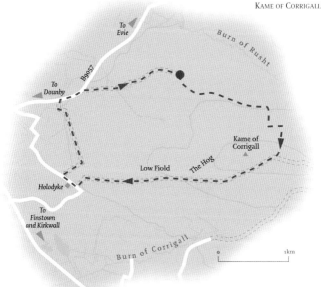

another peat road running from left to right. From here, you have to strike out up the hillside to the summit. It is easier going if you head left for about 50m where another old peat road will help you towards the top.

Although the last section is quite hard work across deep heather, the view as you reach the crest makes it all worthwhile – with the Hoy hills in the distance and the fertile basin in the centre of Orkney's West Mainland below. If you have a picnic with you – and if it is not too windy – this is the place to stop and enjoy the scene.

When it is time to go, walk on across the heather where you will soon come to a track. You cannot miss it as it runs along the southern side of the hill. Turn right and follow it downhill, off the heather and across a narrow field. Keep to the same line along the bottom of the field and follow the track all the way down until it bends left to emerge onto a quiet public road close to the big house at Holodyke.

Turn right. Walk past Holodyke and, soon after, take the first right. Some 250m up the road, take the track that heads left and follow it past a number of new houses, bending left and right until it joins the B9057 Dounby to Evie road. Turn right and walk carefully along this busier (but still pretty quiet) road back to the track to the wind turbine, or turn left for Dounby if you travelled by bus.

◀ The hills of Hoy, viewed from Harray

Wyre

Stronsay Firth

Gairsay

Shapinsay

Shapinsay Sound

Finstown

The Mainland

1

Kirkwall

Stromness

3

Graemsay

2

Scapa Flow

Hoy

Flotta

4

Burray

6

5

South
Ronaldsay

7

Orkney's East Mainland may lack the
famous archaeology found to the west,
but it still has plenty of interest – wild sea
cliffs, long sandy beaches and fascinating
historical sites. There is much to explore.

To the south, the communities of South
Ronaldsay and Burray were transformed
by the wartime decision to link the
islands down the east side of Scapa Flow.
Italian prisoners of war were drafted in to
construct the causeways 'to improve
communication' between the islands,
with the happy coincidence of also
blocking the seaways to enemy

submarines. Today they are known
as the Churchill Barriers, after Winston
Churchill, the Prime Minister who
commissioned them. On the island of
Lamb Holm, a tiny chapel created from
two Nissen huts, known as the Italian
Chapel, remains a testament to the
prisoners' faith and marks their
continuing contribution to Orkney life.

Hunda Causeway ▶

The East Mainland, South Ronaldsay and Burray

Wideford Hill

Distance 10km **Time** 3 hours
Terrain minor roads, moorland paths and
pavement **Maps** OS Explorer 461 and 463
Access Kirkwall is well served by buses

An energetic uphill walk from Kirkwall
with the reward of panoramic views from
the top. On a clear day you can see as far
as Fair Isle to the north and the hills of
Scotland to the south.

The best place to park is at the
Pickaquoy Leisure Centre, known locally
as the Picky Centre. If walking from the
centre of town, however, head west along
the harbourfront, go around the circular
Peedie Sea boating pond and the leisure
centre is ahead in Muddisdale Road.

Start the walk more or less opposite the
main entrance, just as Muddisdale Road
branches off before the car park. Follow

this branch as it bends round to the right,
past the Orcades Hostel, and keep right
when you reach a fork at a row of houses.
After 150m, you will reach the start of the
Muddisdale Footpath and Cycleway on
your left. This meanders up through young
woods to the corner of the golf course and
on up the hill to Sunnybank Road.

After turning left along the road for
200m, take the track on your right up
between fields. Where it joins the public
road, continue uphill until you reach a
small parking bay where the road turns
right. Take the footpath leading left down
through the heather to Wideford Cairn,
crossing another path on the way. The
burial chamber here is unusual because
the structure is not hidden under soil,
and the concentric stone walls give it a
tiered appearance. Access is through a trap

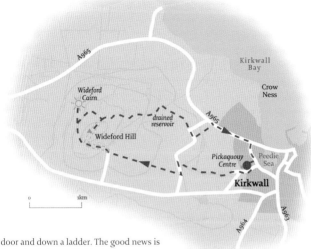

door and down a ladder. The good news is that a torch is provided to help you explore the interior. The bad news is the battery is often flat.

Return back across the field to the intersection of paths. Turn left up the hill, then keep right at a fork, now striking out across the heather to the old hut near the top. Follow the track uphill from the hut, turning right where it meets the road.

On a clear day, the views from Wideford Hill are superb and at the highest point a topograph has been installed, which points out the various hills and islands that can be seen from here. Kirkwall looks different from above with a surprising number of trees nestling between the houses. You can see how much of the town is built on land reclaimed from the sea; in the 12th century, the Vikings built their cathedral on the water's edge. Today

it stands 350m from the harbour!

The journey home begins by heading downhill in a northeasterly direction, past the track to the old hut on your left, until the road ends just beyond. A path wends through the heather towards the big wind turbine below. Once out of the heather, the path leads onto a right of way, dropping down past the old Wideford Reservoir, now drained, and along the track to the public road.

Turn right and, after 250m, take the grassy path which goes sharp left downhill. It emerges onto the pavement by the main road out of Kirkwall. Turn right and walk down to the roundabout. A right turn here takes you onto Pickaquoy Road and back to the leisure centre.

Dingieshowe to the Point of Ayre

Distance 11km **Time** 3 hours 30 (there and back) **Terrain** sandy beaches and coastal paths **Map** OS Explorer 461 **Access** buses from Kirkwall to Deerness will stop at Dingieshowe on request

A peaceful walk along attractive beaches and low-lying cliffs teeming with birdlife. Along the way there are wonderful views of Orkney's eastern headlands and out to the RSPB-owned island of Copinsay.

There is a small parking area by the public toilets at Dingieshowe on the A960. Wooden steps lead over the dunes. Look right to see the remains of the broch from which the beach gets its name.

Dingieshowe is a modern corruption of Tings Howe – *ting* being the Old Norse word for 'assembly' – and it is thought the broch was used as a meeting place in Viking times. There are two bays here, Dingieshowe to the right and Taracliff to the left, although only the latter is named on the OS map.

The walk begins by heading left along Taracliff Bay and up the steps at the far end onto the coastal path. As you round the headland you will pass the Muckle Castle, a volcanic plug of markedly different rock to the surrounding sandstone cliffs. From here, the coastal path becomes narrow and you may prefer to take the grass track that heads inland through the field gate opposite the Muckle Castle. (If you do, follow it uphill until it becomes a public road leading to a junction with the A960. Turn right,

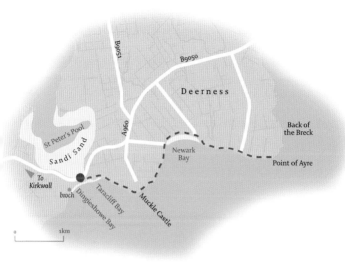

Deerness

B9051

B9050

A960

St Peter's Pool

Sandi Sand

To Kirkwall

broch

Dingieshowe Bay

Taracliff Bay

Newark Bay

Muckle Castle

Back of the Breck

Point of Ayre

0   1km

signposted 'Geo', and the minor road will take you to the Deerness slipway.)

If you stay by the coast, the path will also take you to the slip, but it is less well used and fairly rough in places. The routes converge at Newark Bay, overlooking the slip. From here you can enjoy a fine view along the beach and over to the uninhabited island of Copinsay, the smaller Horse of Copinsay and the Holms, which now collectively make up an RSPB Bird Reserve. It is also a good spot to look for the mermaid who is said to have visited Newark Bay for several summers (although if you spot her, you will be the first person to do so in over 120 years).

Continue along the beach, or on the track behind it, to a small parking area at

the far end. From here the path is signed to Aikerskaill Road, and leads above the shore for just over 1km to yet another car park. Beyond is a metal gate opening onto a wide grassy strip between the fields and the shore, with a rustic wooden sign showing the way to the Point of Ayre.

The path will take you past the three large wind turbines and, a little further on, to a headland with an information board about the islands offshore. This is as close as you can get to Copinsay without a boat and as far as you can go along the coastline without having to climb fences repeatedly. From here, retrace your steps to Dingieshowe to collect your car or hail a bus back to town.

◀ Looking out to Copinsay

The Mull Head and the Covenanters' Memorial

Distance 9km **Time** 3 hours
Terrain coastal and inland paths, farm
tracks; steep, narrow climb up the cliff to
the Brough of Deerness
Map OS Explorer 461 **Access** bus from
Kirkwall to Deerness stops at the
Lighthouse Corner, 2.5km from the start

**Explore the local nature reserve on the
eastern headland of Deerness, passing a
spectacular collapsed cave and an old
Viking settlement. Then take the path to
a memorial to the Covenanters who died
at sea, trapped in the bowels of their ship.**

To reach the start, follow signs to
Deerness and drive as far east as possible,
turning north at Skaill to the car park for
The Gloup. You might first want to cross
the road to the interpretation centre
which is full of useful information about
the Mull Head Reserve. Then take the path
from the car park towards the sea.

You will soon come to the viewing
platforms for The Gloup, a huge hole in
the ground caused by the partial collapse
of a sea cave. 'Gloup' derives from the Old
Norse *gluppa*, meaning 'chasm'.

Beyond is a gate which leads left to the
Brough of Deerness. There is a steep
descent to the base of the Brough with a
steeper, narrow and exposed path up the
other side, although a chain handrail
helps you climb.

The ruins of a 10th-century chapel are
visible, but archaeologists believe there
was a large settlement here during the
11th and 12th centuries with perhaps as
many as 30 structures on the summit.

From the Brough continue to follow the
path north, past deep geos, to the Mull
Head itself. This headland is battered by
storms in winter, but alive with seabirds
in summer. Sea pinks and spring squill
thrive on the cliff edges, and the colour

THE MULL HEAD AND THE COVENANTERS' MEMORIAL

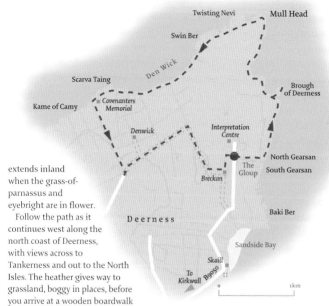

extends inland when the grass-of-parnassus and eyebright are in flower.

Follow the path as it continues west along the north coast of Deerness, with views across to Tankerness and out to the North Isles. The heather gives way to grassland, boggy in places, before you arrive at a wooden boardwalk with a sign pointing inland. This offers a shortcut home if you want one (at the far end of the path, aim for a little wind turbine on the crest of the hill; from here you'll see the car park), but the path to the Covenanters' Memorial lies across the boardwalk and on along the coast. Footbridges help you to cross awkward sections and the path runs between the field boundaries and clifftops.

Around 200 Covenanters drowned in 1679 when their ship, the *Crown of London*, was smashed on the rocks below the memorial. They were locked below decks while being transported to the American

colonies after being taken prisoner following the Battle of Bothwell Brig.

Walk inland for 1km to a parking area, then go left on the rough path beside the farm track, continuing straight ahead where the track turns left to Denwick farm. After 750m, you come to a junction with the track for East Denwick. Turn right and walk for 250m to the gate onto a path that runs straight uphill to a little wind turbine, where you can see your car over to the left. The path turns left to drop downhill past the farm buildings at Breckan, before turning left again, then right to reach the car park.

◀ Deerness cliffs

Burray and Hunda

Distance 13.5km **Time** 4 hours 30
Terrain minor roads, farm tracks and
grassy paths **Map** OS Explorer 461
Access bus from Kirkwall to Burray village

**From the highest point on Burray you can
see all the Churchill Barriers connecting
the islands down Orkney's east coast, as
well as the causeway to Hunda. It makes
the island accessible at all tides but is
best avoided in bad weather.**

Until the Churchill Barriers were built
during the Second World War, Burray
depended on ferries to link with the rest
of Orkney. The old pier is a good place to
start the walk and there is plenty of
parking in front of the Sands Hotel.

As you face the pier, set off along the
road to the right, then walk 100m across

the grass near the shore to a small
parking area. There is a right of way
between the houses opposite which leads
up the side of two gardens, emerging onto
a public road just above a corrugated
workshop. After turning left and walking
past the speed limit signs, take the first
right and follow the road uphill. Leave the
road when it bends to the right and head
straight on up the track between a fence
and drystane dyke. Turn left where it joins
a farm track, then left again before
bending sharp right to follow the track to
the trig point at the top.

From here, you can see all four
Churchill Barriers which were built to
protect Scapa Flow. There is a glorious
view to St Margaret's Hope over your
left shoulder and round to Copinsay
behind your right.

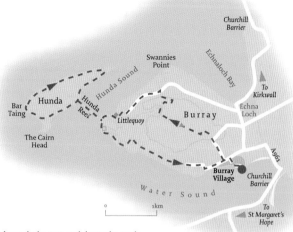

Go through the gate and down the track across the heather towards Hunda, turning right where it meets another track at the bottom. You might want to explore the site of an anti-aircraft battery ahead of you, but to continue the walk turn right at the grassy crossroads by the old concrete roller. Go up to the gate, then turn left to walk down the track to the surfaced road.

Another left turn will take you to the farm at Littlequoy. Sheep are grazed on Hunda and, if there is anyone in the house, it is courteous to check if it is okay to cross. Then head through the steading and over the causeway. At the far side, go left past the quarry which provided the stone for the causeway. A path, faint in places, runs the whole way round the island. Arctic terns nest in great numbers on Hunda, so stick to the path to avoid disturbing them in the nesting season.

From the north end, you can see Holm Sound, the channel used by the German submarine *U-47* to enter Scapa Flow and sink the *HMS Royal Oak* in October 1939 with the loss of more than 830 lives.

Once back across the causeway, head right on the faint path to the old ruin covered with lichen. Approximately 400m further on, by the low ruins of another building, step over the fence and go through the gate into the field. Walk to the top right-hand corner and through the left-hand gate. Turn right to meet a farm track which will lead you across the grassy hillside. This track joins the public road to return to the corrugated shed at the top of the right of way. A right turn will take you back to the pier.

◀ Burray ruin

Kirkhouse and Grimness

Distance 10km **Time** 3 hours 30
Terrain coastal paths and minor roads,
linked by 1km of pathless rough ground
Map OS Explorer 461 **Access** bus from
Kirkwall to St Margaret's Hope, 4km from
the start

Starting and finishing near standing
stones erected 5000 years apart, this
walk along the delightful east coast of
South Ronaldsay goes past the wreck
of the *SS Irene*, a reminder of one of
Orkney's most tragic maritime disasters.

St Peter's Kirk overlooks the picturesque
beach at Newark Bay. Its generous car park
makes a perfect start point. To find it, turn
off the A961 at the war memorial above
St Margaret's Hope. Go straight over at
the crossroads – you'll find the kirk at the
bottom of the hill.

Set off down the track towards
the beach for a few paces until a gap
between the wall and the fencepost
allows you through to the path. Go past
the old fisherman's store and the circular
base of an 18th-century windmill, and
walk above the shore. You will pass a
modern monolith, called the Millennium
Stone, as you follow the curve of the
bay, passing through gates as you
come to them.

After Manse Bay, take care getting
round the end of the fence immediately
before the derelict cottage, but thereafter
the going is easy along a grassy farm
track above low cliffs. Look out for
circular hollow in the grass just after the
track down from Dyke End, evidence of an
old lead mine below. After the next field
gate, with a polite notice to keep dogs on

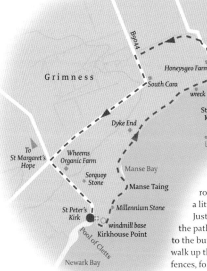

Grimness

B9044

Kirk Geo

Honeysgeo Farm

South Cara

wreck

Grim Ness

Stack of Kame

Dyke End

0   1km

To St Margaret's Hope

Wheems Organic Farm

Sorquoy Stone

Manse Bay

Manse Taing

Millennium Stone

St Peter's Kirk

windmill base
Kirkhouse Point

Pool of Cletts

Newark Bay

leads, you will see the remains of the *SS Irene* below the cliff.

The freighter broke down in the Pentland Firth during a violent storm in 1969, and the Longhope lifeboat overturned while trying to reach her. All eight crew-members of the lifeboat were drowned while the *Irene* eventually drifted ashore, allowing her crew to be rescued from the cliff.

The path leads round onto the Grimness promontory. Follow the coastline to reach a gate through to a farm track. Turn right onto the minor road below Honeysgeo Farm, which leads

round the bay and inland to a little bridge with stone walls.

Just before the bridge, cut left onto the path past young trees, sticking close to the burn. Go through the gate, then walk up the rough grass between the fences, following the water upstream. It is quite hard work for the next 1km, but keep going to the road at the top, turning left through two gates to get onto the road itself. Be careful of the crude catch on the second gate – it can be a finger crusher.

Turn left along the road, following it round to the right and all the way back to the crossroads, where a left turn leads downhill to the car park. Below Wheems Organic Farm, look left to see one of the tallest standing stones in Orkney. The Sorquoy Stone (also known as the Papley Stone) is over 4m high. It has been here for 5000 years more than the Millennium Stone which is just visible on the shoreline below.

◀ Kirkhouse, South Ronaldsay

The Hope to Hoxa Head

Distance 12km **Time** 3 hours 30
Terrain minor roads, farmland with
livestock, and coastal paths
Map OS Explorer 461 **Access** bus from
Kirkwall to St Margaret's Hope

**A brisk walk from the picturesque village
known locally as 'The Hope' to explore an
exposed headland which once bristled
with guns to guard the British fleet.**

Traffic through St Margaret's Hope can
be heavy at ferry times, but otherwise the
village is quiet and peaceful. Its little
streets are well worth exploring, with
shops, galleries, an award-winning
restaurant and even a blacksmith's
museum waiting to be discovered.

Park in Cromarty Square on the B9043
just before the road turns left to the ferry
terminal. Walk towards the sea and turn
left. Take the first left, over the brow of
the hill and straight over the crossroads
by Heatherum Farm. Go up the concrete

tracks and then the farm track to the top,
where a grass path forks left. Follow this
path downhill, bending right, then past
two houses to the bottom. Turn left onto
more concrete tracks and walk left along
the shore.

Step up off the beach just before the
cottage, walking outside the rope which
marks the garden boundary, and onto the
track round the bay. The mound above the
house at the far end of the bay is said to
be the burial place of the legendary
10th-century Earl of Orkney, Thorfinn
Skullsplitter, after whom both a ferry and
a locally-brewed beer are named.

The track bends left at the end of the
loch, then right to lead up to the public
road. Walk over the crest of the hill and
turn left at the lopsided crossroads. This
quiet road now runs almost the length of
the peninsula, past the Tapestry Gallery to
the Hoxa Tearooms.

Here, the road becomes a farm track and

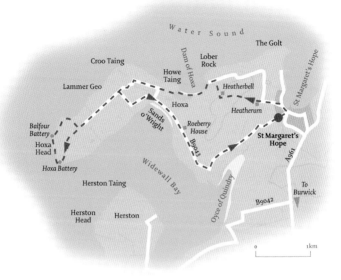

Water Sound

The Golt

St Margaret's Hope

Croo Taing

Lober Rock

Howe Taing

Dam of Hoxa

Heatherbell

Lammer Geo

Hoxa

Heatherum

Sands o'Wright

Roeberry House

St Margaret's Hope

Balfour Battery

B9043

Hoxa Head

Hoxa Battery

Widewall Bay

A961

To Burwick

Oyce of Quindry

Herston Taing

B9042

Herston Head

Herston

0   1km

heads straight over the brow to look out to the Pentland Firth. Head left where the track joins another and walk down to the Hoxa Battery. To reach the lookout posts and the clifftop path you will have to cross a barbed wire fence, so you may prefer to walk along the inside of the fence to reach the Balfour Battery 500m to your right.

On the way, you will pass trenches, shaped like two giant horseshoes, where the guns were situated during the First World War. The Balfour Battery guarded the boom nets and looks over towards the equally well-fortified island of Flotta.

Shortly after the last of the wartime buildings, the path rounds a low

headland and soon you will see a gate to your right, leading inland to the tearoom.

After a quick refreshment, head back along the public road and turn right by the flooded quarry. At the bottom of the hill, turn left and follow the road down to the bay. The beach is called the Sands o'Wright, best known for the annual Boys' Ploughing Match which takes place here in August. Using miniature ploughs, local youngsters create furrows on a small patch of beach under the watchful gaze of their fathers and grandfathers.

The road leads on past Roeberry House, bending sharp left at Quindry, to bring you back to the village through Cromarty Square.

◂ Searchlight emplacement, Hoxa

Olav's Wood

Distance 1.5km **Time** 30 minutes (there and back) **Terrain** Grass paths, uneven, slippery in places **Map** OS Explorer 461 **Access** no public transport and very limited parking at the entrance

More of an exploration than an expedition, this short walk meanders through a small but varied tree plantation alongside a trickling burn. It's a combination which makes for a delightful half-hour stroll. The kids will love it!

Olav's Wood has been slowly developing on the banks of Oback Burn since the 1970s. A typically sparse Orkney hillside has been transformed by thoughtful planting and dogged determination, not least by Olav Dennison after whom it is named.

To find it, head south on the A961 from St Margaret's Hope, turning left after 7km at the Windwick signpost. Olav's Wood is 700m along the road, on the right. Park in the spaces provided and not in the nearby passing place.

As soon as you enter the woodland, a network of paths lead into the trees. The youngest trees are nearest the road and you can see the efforts which have been made to keep the coarse grass from choking the saplings. There is a mix of deciduous and evergreen species, with the North American sitka spruce and lodgepole pines providing shelter for other varieties. Look out too for young monkey puzzles, growing stoically a long way from their native Chile.

The paths are named after various people who have been instrumental in

42

◀ In Olav's Wood

the development of the woodland, but you need not worry about which to take. Generally, head downhill and explore the different avenues as they take your fancy. Be warned that some of the paths can be very slippery and children should be supervised, especially when close to the water.

A little footbridge over the burn marks the point at which the paths converge, where the woodland is at its narrowest, beside a hedge of rosa rugosa. Once over the burn, go left into a dense area of spruce trees called Helen's Wood, after Helen Manson who first started planting here. Teapots hang from branches as nesting boxes and you may come across nets – used for bird ringing – which you

are asked not to touch, even when they are furled up for storage.

As the path descends by the burn, there are several pools and cascades, little bridges and a dam, which enhance the charm of the lower stretches of the woodland. The vegetation is more open here, and planted with an exotic variety of shrubs and small trees. You will know when you have reached the bottom of the glen when the path crosses a small bridge to a bench. This is a lovely spot to sit and contemplate how Orkney might once have looked before our forefathers stripped away the trees to create the landscape we know today. To return home, just follow the burn back up to the entrance, exploring more as you go.

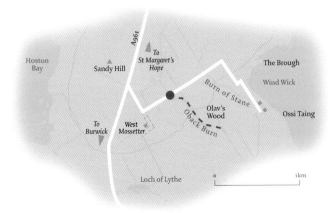

Hoy takes its name from the Old Norse *Háey*, meaning 'High Island', and boasts Orkney's three highest hills, as well as some of the tallest sea cliffs in Britain. The iconic rock stack The Old Man of Hoy and the naval base at Lyness attract visitors from around the world. Flotta, named by the Vikings as 'the Flat Island', is home to the oil terminal whose flare stack lights up the winter skies. It is also rich in wartime heritage. Graemsay sits amid turbulent currents between Hoy and Stromness, its lighthouses guiding ships safely into harbour. It is one of just three populated islands in Orkney without a roll-on, roll-off ferry service.

The South Isles

Flotta

Distance 14km **Time** 4 hours 30
Terrain quiet roads, rough coastal
paths with several stiles to cross
Map OS Explorer 462 **Access** ferry from
Lyness, as well as from Houton – which
is served by limited bus services from
Kirkwall and Stromness

**Many people are put off visiting Flotta
because of the oil terminal which
dominates the island. They miss out on
amazing wartime heritage, wonderful
moor and heathlands, interesting
wildlife on land and water, and sea-level
views of the neighbouring islands. Take
your binoculars.**

Turn right at the top of the pier, and
right again to follow the road beside the
sea. Ahead is the impressive ruin of the
wartime cinema set among conifer trees
planted by naval ratings in the Second
World War. The trees provide a rare
habitat in Orkney for birds like the robin,
chaffinch and goldcrest.

The pier to the west is named after
Flotta-born Forby Sutherland who sailed
with Captain Cook. He died in Botany Bay
in 1770 and was the first British subject
to be buried on Australian soil.
Sutherland Point in Botany Bay was
named in his honour.

Following the shoreline, the road
leads past the disused airstrip, with
views across to Lyness and the two
Martello Towers which were built to
protect Longhope Bay during the
Napoleonic Wars.

The road then bends left, above the
wartime gun batteries at The Neb, and
continues for 700m to the derelict

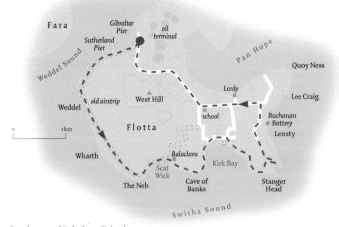

Fara

Gibraltar Pier

oil terminal

Sutherland Pier

Pan Hope

Quoy Ness

Weddel Sound

Lurdy

Lee Craig

Weddel

old airstrip

West Hill

school

Buchanan Battery

Flotta

Lensty

Wharth

Balaclava

Kirk Bay

Scat Wick

The Neb

Cave of Banks

Stanger Head

Swítha Sound

0   1km

farmhouse of Balaclava. Take the grass path leading down to the water's edge on your right, then go left onto the coastal path. For the next 1km the path is easily followed round the headland, but you will be required to cross stiles at several points where coastal erosion has made the path impassable.

Soon you will emerge onto a quiet public road at Kirk Bay. Fork right at the junction, and walk behind the church to the end of the cemetery wall. Take the rough track on your right down to the sea and continue on the coastal path round towards the headland.

The ground becomes rougher as you near the Port War Signal Station on top of the hill. The path up to the signal station may be hard to find, but it is easy to pick your own route across the heather. Behind the signal station a track leads past a flooded quarry and joins another

track where a right turn will take you down to the Stanger Head.

Retrace your steps back up the slope and, with the flooded quarry to your left, follow the track inland as it heads gently over the hill. You will soon see the Buchanan Battery on the shore, with a track leading down to allow a closer look. The walk continues along the public road, turning left at the T-junction.

A further 300m on, a track leads down to the right which will take you to the Lurdy Centre, a delightfully informal heritage centre next to the shop and post office. From here, the route home is easy to find by following the main road back to the terminal. At the highest point, the road affords a good view over the oil terminal and beyond, the only opportunity on land to see Stromness and Kirkwall at the same time.

◀ Flotta shoreline

Graemsay

**Distance 9.5km Time 4 hours
Terrain rough coastal path, some open
farmland Map OS Explorer 463
Access passenger ferry from Stromness
and Moaness**

**Stick to the coast around the tranquil
island of Graemsay which sits between
Stromness and Hoy. It has abandoned
crofts, derelict boats, a wartime battery,
lighthouses, seabirds and wildflowers.
Above all it has peace, quiet and
wonderful views.**

Most walkers using the ferry called
Graemsay are heading for Hoy and never
set foot on the island it is named after, so
it is likely you will have the coastline all
to yourself. Walk up from the pier for
200m until the road turns sharply inland,
then take the rough path to your left. This
will lead you along the shore, past the
ruined croft buildings at Scarrataing and
round the southern corner of the island.

As you draw near the old church,
take the wooden steps onto the foreshore
to avoid a section of rough and boggy
ground. A stile at the far end of the
cemetery wall invites you to climb into
the field, but there is no need to. The path
continues close to the water, rough in
places but easy to negotiate. It runs along
the shoreline to a row of boat nousts
beside a crumbling stone shelter.

Most nousts in Orkney are empty
these days, but the remains of an old
open boat can still be seen here with the
winch used to haul it ashore. Further
along there is a marker post beside a
small gate. Ignore the arrow pointing
inland and continue along the coastline.
There is not much of a path, but it is easy
to find your way between the fence and
the low clifftops.

Take care where the cliffs get a little
higher, and you might have to drop down
onto the rocks to avoid livestock as you

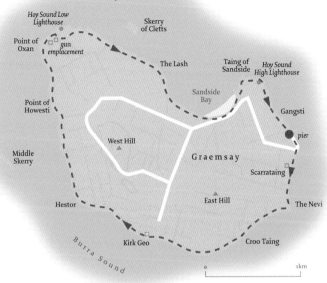

near the wartime buildings and lighthouse. The Graemsay Battery was built to strengthen the Second World War anti-motor-torpedo-boat defences. The twin searchlight structures are highly unusual and it is rare to find a gun emplacement with no overhead cover.

The Lighthouse, Hoy Sound Low, is one of a pair which together lead vessels safely through the Hoy Sound channel. If the tide is out, shards of pottery – part of the cargo of the SS *Albion*, wrecked here in 1866 – can be found among the rocks on the Point of Oxan below the searchlight buildings.

Walk round the lighthouse wall and onto the track leading uphill. Take the field gate on your left and cross to the far side. Turn right and enjoy a delightful walk along the coast to Sandside Bay, close to the other lighthouse, Hoy Sound High. On the way you'll pass an old jetty, the island's closest landing point to Stromness.

At Sandside, cross the impressive 19th-century pier – built for the construction of the lighthouses – and look for the white maerl (like coral) brought ashore in the currents. Follow the path round to the lighthouse, dropping down onto the rocks until you are past the perimeter wall, for the last short stretch back to the ferry pier.

The Old Man of Hoy

Distance 9.5km **Time** 3 hours (there and back) **Terrain** hillside path (muddy in places), then well-maintained footpath **Map** OS Explorer 462 **Access** passenger ferry from Stromness to Moaness (at the north of Hoy) with a minibus service to Rackwick meeting the mid-morning ferry in the summer and by arrangement over the winter – booking is advisable; if you walk from the ferry at Moaness, it will add a further 6.5km each way

It is hard to beat the footpath to the Old Man of Hoy, climbing steeply from the remote and beautiful Rackwick Bay, then across the heather-clad hillside to the most famous rock stack in the country.

From the large car park at the end of the Rackwick road, set off along the second track on your left, signposted for the Old Man of Hoy, and follow it towards the north end of the bay, between the crofthouses, over the cattle grid and down towards the shore.

Follow the track as it bends to the right and climbs up the hillside, stepping onto the grass when the track bends back round towards a private house. From here the path is fainter across the grass, but leads to a well-trodden footpath further up the hillside where you turn left.

Take note of the stone buildings, roofed with turf, which you will pass on your way back. Once a croft, it is now the Cra'as Nest, an informal and informative museum which shows how life was once lived in this isolated valley.

The path leads across and up the hillside. This has been a popular walk

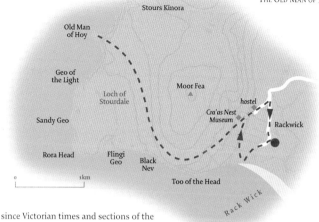

Stours Kinora

Old Man
of Hoy

Geo of
the Light

Moor Fea

Loch of
Stourdale

hostel

Cra'as Nest
Museum

Rackwick

Sandy Geo

Rora Head

Flingi
Geo

Black
Nev

Too of the Head

0   1km

Rack Wick

since Victorian times and sections of the route were paved in stone, with some stretches still remaining, including the occasional set of stone steps.

Once you have rounded the shoulder of Moor Fea, the path veers away from the cliffs. Soon the Loch of Stourdale comes into view, then the Old Man, although at this stage you can only see the very top of his head. A pale pink path lies ahead across the moor, a stark contrast to the heather and stone-clad moorland on either side.

In the breeding season, be on your guard for bonxies aggressively protecting their nests and young. You will see more of the Old Man as you get nearer, but it is only when you reach the top of the cliff that you can fully appreciate its height and scale. The winds can be gusty and unpredictable near the cliff, so take great care and stay well back from the edge.

The 137m high stack was first climbed in 1966 when Chris Bonington, Rustie

Baillie and Tom Patey took three days to reach the summit. Most climbers manage it in a few hours these days before abseiling back down, but in 2008 three climbers base-jumped from the top. It took seven hours to go up, and just ten seconds to descend.

The walk back to the car park involves retracing your steps across the moor, round the shoulder of Moor Fea and down the hillside overlooking Rackwick Bay. This time, do not turn right onto the track down towards the shore, but head along below the Cra'as Nest.

Carry on down to the cluster of houses at the end of the path, where there are two other heritage buildings to explore. From here, head past the phonebox, turning right where you can, onto the road back to the car park. Leave some time to explore the beach before heading for home.

Lyrawa Hill and Scad Head

Distance 4km **Time** 1 hour 30
Terrain steep waymarked path
Map OS Explorer 462 **Access** no public
transport to the start

This is a walk of two halves: downhill
and uphill. Down to the ruins of a
wartime gun battery which once guarded
the entrance to Scapa Flow, then back
to the grave of poor Betty Corrigall,
buried between parishes for her sins.
This may be a short walk, but it will
test your knees.

The Lyrawa Viewpoint overlooks Scapa
Flow, roughly halfway between Hoy's two
ferry piers. It is signposted from the
B9047, and a rough track allows you to
take your car to the viewpoint where there
is plenty of space to leave it.

Located on the site of an old anti-
aircraft battery, the viewpoint provides a
glorious view over the Bring Deeps and
Scapa Flow. From the information panel at
the viewpoint, head left and walk below
the concrete gun emplacement to pick up
the first of the marker posts which lead
down across the hill, keeping you above
the steepest part of the hillside.

The path brings you out on the line of
an old railway track which runs down the
slope. Unusually for a military site of this
scale, the battery at Scad Head had no
road to it, so it was supplied by a narrow
gauge railway. Cables lowered the
carriages down the hill and pulled them
back up again.

Turn right at the railway track and head
down to the bottom of the hill. The first
buildings are the remains of the old
accommodation camp. The path then
heads round behind the camp, over a little
bridge, to the gun battery at Scad Head
where the buildings have survived pretty
much intact.

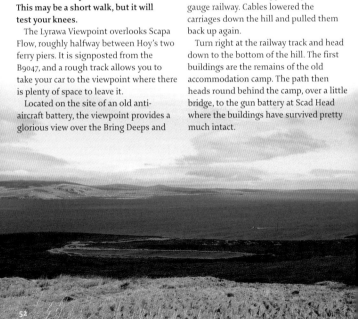

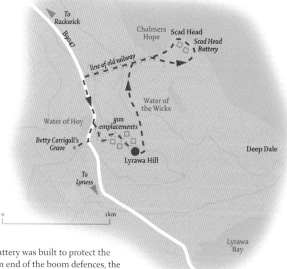

The battery was built to protect the southern end of the boom defences, the nets which were suspended across the channel to prevent attack. The shore is littered with debris from the war, making it a great place to explore. Look for the cast-iron communication cable sheathing, anti-submarine nets and the chassis of an old railway carriage.

Return back round the bay to the track and follow it straight up the hill, past the winding wheel which used to haul the carriages, and turn left onto the road. Walk 150m beyond the track to the viewpoint, turning right onto the path leading across to Betty Corrigall's grave.

In the 1770s this poor woman, unmarried and pregnant, took her own life after being abandoned by her lover. Denied a Christian burial, she was interred in unconsecrated ground on the boundary between the parishes. Her resting place was unmarked and forgotten until two men out cutting peat came across her preserved corpse in 1933. She was soon reburied, again with her grave unmarked, but during the war morbid curiosity got the better of soldiers stationed on the island and she was regularly exhumed. It took until 1976 for a gravestone to be erected and fenced off and for a burial service to be performed at the lonely spot.

From her grave it is only a short walk back to the starting point at the Lyrawa Hill viewpoint.

◀ View over Water of the Wicks and the Bring Deeps

53

Lyness and Wee Fea

Distance 6km **Time** 3 hours
Terrain public roads and old military
tracks **Map** OS Explorer 462 **Access** regular
ferries from Houton to Lyness

**Explore a wartime base which played a
vital part in the battles for the North
Atlantic and North Sea before heading
up to the Communication Centre and
secret underground storage tanks on
the hill.**

Stepping off the ferry in Lyness you will
face the Scapa Flow Visitor Centre. Once a
wartime pumping station, it is now a
fascinating (and free) museum with
artifacts and information from both
World Wars.

Walk along the main road heading away
from the visitor centre, passing the
remains of old wartime piers, with
another on the opposite shore. The huge

iron shed dates from the First World War,
and was converted into the Royal Naval
Recreational Centre in 1939 when Lyness
became the base for the Home Fleet. It
housed the NAAFI, shops, restaurants,
billiards room and a 900-seat cinema.

Follow the road as it leaves the shore
and turns inland. In the distance is the
hill of Wee Fea, dominated by the Naval
HQ and Communication Centre near the
summit. Cross the B9047 and head up the
minor road, signposted to Wee Fea, with
the Hoy Hotel to your right.

After the road crosses a cattle grid by
the corner of the plantation, it becomes a
rough track and heads uphill until it turns
left to the Communication Centre.
Continue along the track for 200m to a
picnic area with views across Scapa Flow
and the Pentland Firth.

Return past the Communication Centre

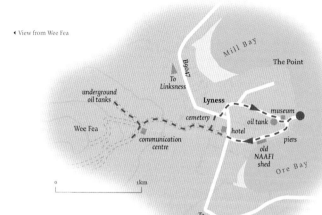

◀ View from Wee Fea

Map labels:

Mill Bay

The Point

B9047

To
Linksness

underground
oil tanks

Lyness

cemetery

museum

oil tank

hotel

piers

Wee Fea

communication
centre

old
NAAFI
shed

Ore Bay

0   1km

To
Longhope

B9047

but instead of going downhill, turn left just before the sign pointing to Wee Fea. Almost immediately, there is a less distinct path which forks to the right across the hillside leading, after 150m, to the entrance to a complex of wartime underground oil storage tanks. These were constructed because the tanks at Lyness were vulnerable to attack. The smell of heavy oil still hangs in the air and, although the entrance is padlocked, you can generate an impressive echo from the gates.

Head back downhill and over the cattle grid. As you walk towards the Hoy Hotel, look for the path on the left leading to the Lyness Naval Cemetery, where more than 600 wartime casualties of various nationalities are buried.

Leave the cemetery by the opposite gate and turn right along the B9047, then go

left at the electricity sub-station. As you walk along the track, you are passing between the gas decontamination station on your left and the original communication centre, surrounded by a blast wall, on your right.

The track rejoins the public road at a minor crossroads. Go straight across and head down past the brick shed which once served as the naval base's squash courts. Where the public road goes left, fork right onto the track and follow it down past the oil tank to the visitor centre. There should be time for a cup of tea in the café before catching the ferry or setting off to explore the rest of the island.

Cantick Head

Distance 4km **Time** 1 hour 30
Terrain minor road and grassland paths,
soft in places **Map** OS Explorer 462
Access no public transport to the start

**Cantick Head offers superb views over
the Pentland Firth and is one of the best
places in Orkney for whale watching.
It's not the best walk on a wild day,
but in fine weather it makes for a
delightful outing.**

This corner of Orkney will always be
associated with the Longhope Lifeboat
Disaster of 1969. All eight crew members,
drawn from four local families, died trying
to help a ship in trouble in the Pentland
Firth. There is a moving memorial in the
cemetery close to the start of the walk and
a magnificent museum in the old lifeboat

shed at Brims, near the causeway linking
South Walls to the rest of Hoy.

To reach the starting point, drive
south from the Lyness ferry terminal on
the B9047 for 10km. After crossing
The Ayre, with sea on both sides of the
road, fork right for a further 4.5km to a
small sandy beach. The walk begins from
the car park at the far end.

Turn right onto the lighthouse road
with the water on your left. Opposite the
navigation beacon offshore, the road
turns up to the lighthouse. Look for the
stile to help you cross the fence and
onto the indistinct path which will
take you onto the open pasture beyond
the lighthouse.

Minke and pilot whales are often seen
hunting in the currents and eddies

◀ Cantick Head Lighthouse

offshore, and you might even spot an orca if you are particularly lucky. Basking sharks and dolphins are not unknown here.

The path continues along the top of the cliffs towards the end of a drystane dyke. Here, you will see the only square burial chamber so far discovered in Orkney (although it is believed to be an Iron Age modification of an earlier round burial chamber). As the cliffs fall away, the path leads down to a low rocky shoreline and Hesti Geo Broch. Now just a steep rocky mound, this would have been a mighty tower two thousand years ago.

Soon you will arrive at the steep-sided West Geo. The path turns inland here to a gate by the dyke and then round the side of a field and back to the car park. If you would like to extend the walk a little, however, go back out onto the road, turning left this time and along the beach to the cemetery at Osmundwall.

According to legend this is where one of the best known Vikings, Earl Sigurd Hlodvirsson, also known as Sigurd the Stout, was forced to choose between converting to Christianity or being put to death. All of Orkney is said to have embraced the faith after his baptism! There is a carved stone bench at the cemetery depicting the story and, not far away, the memorial to the lifeboatmen who died in the Longhope Disaster.

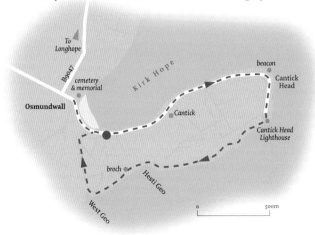

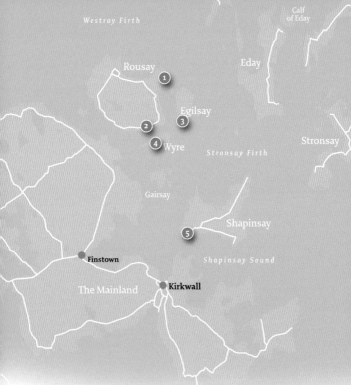

Orkney's Inner North Isles are served by ferries, shaped like landing craft, which shuttle to and fro throughout the day. The boat from Tingwall runs to the three islands of Rousay, Egilsay and Wyre.

Rousay's distinctive terraced hillsides were fashioned by glaciers and its southern shores are dotted with spectacular ruins dating across thousands of years. Make sure you visit the Midhowe Chambered Cairn and the other sites close by. Egilsay and Wyre may be among Orkney's smaller island communities, but each can boast ancient sites of the highest order, St Magnus' Church in Egilsay and Cubbie Roo's Castle in Wyre.

Shapinsay is a short hop from Kirkwall by boat and has one of the prettiest harbours in the country. The farmland is green and fertile, and produces some of the best livestock in Orkney.

Shapinsay Harbour ▸

The Inner North Isles

Faraclett Head

Distance **3.5km** Time **1 hour 30**
Terrain **waymarked path and farmland**
Map **OS Explorer 464** Access **ferry from Tingwall to Rousay; bus service on Thursday only which stops at Faraclett if requested; booking must be made the day before**

Head out across the northeast corner of Rousay, over coastal heath and grassland, to the highest point on Faraclett Head with views that get bigger and better the further you go.

From the ferry pier, drive north for 4km. After the road bends sharp right, then sharp left, take the next turning on the right and follow it until you reach the end of the surfaced road. The parking area is clearly marked at the bottom of the farm track to the left.

The path sets off up the hill across two waymarked stiles. Once over the second stile, bear right over the brow to a kissing gate in the far fence. Do not go through

the gate at this stage (it is used on the way back), but walk uphill on the farm track – the exposed rock flagstones make a perfect road surface – to a gate at the top of the field. Go left. From here, the path is clearly marked by posts, the first of which is set against the skyline ahead of you.

There is a good example of Rousay's terraced hillsides across the valley. The terraces are often misinterpreted as agricultural, but were created by glaciers during the last ice age. You will pass a couple of degraded burial mounds on your way to a marker post mounted on a drystane plinth. From here, the views over the North Isles begin to unfold.

In front of you is Westray with the Noup Head Lighthouse a white dot on the western headland. Where the path bears right, it is marked by posts set well back up the hillside. Do not be tempted to walk any lower down the slope. The high overhanging cliffs, hidden from view beneath the grassy slopes, are eroding

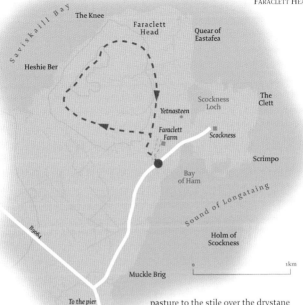

with every northwestern gale and should be treated with great respect.

The marker posts lead you to a square stone cairn which marks the summit of Faraclett Head. The view is wonderful and, on a clear day, even Fair Isle is visible 80km to the northeast.

Follow the path down the hill to the marker post. From there it leads to the right, onto the more cultivated land lower down the slope, with views over the Scockness Loch and the ayre which separates the loch from the sea.

Go through the gate and across the pasture to the stile over the drystane dyke. The path leads generally south towards Faraclett Farm, running more or less parallel to the dyke, with another ladder stile to cross on the way. Look for the substantial standing stone at the bottom of the field below. This is the Yetnasteen (from the Old Norse for 'Giant Stone') which, legend has it, nips down to the loch for a quick drink at Hogmanay.

The path leads onto a rough tractor track from where you will see the waymarked gate you passed on the outbound leg of the walk. From here it is a simple matter of following your steps back over the two stiles and down the hill to the parking area.

Rousay and Blotchnie Fiold

Distance 7.5km **Time** 2 hours 30
Terrain moorland path, boggy in places,
and minor roads; some pathless ground
Map OS Explorer 464 **Access** regular ferry
services from Tingwall to Rousay

**Walk up from the pier on Rousay to an
RSPB Reserve above Trumland House and
gardens. The views are wonderful and the
birds can be spectacular.**

There is no need to take a vehicle on the
boat for this walk, but if you do, park it
opposite the ferry ramp and set off on
foot uphill past the telephone box.
Bear left at the war memorial and follow
the road to the junction by Trumland
House gates.

Trumland House was built by General
Sir Frederick Traill-Burroughs in 1873 on
his retirement from military service.
Known locally as 'the Little General'
because of his short stature and
overbearing nature, Burroughs had been
part of the heroic Thin Red Line at the
Battle of Alama in the Crimea and was
one of the last defenders of Lucknow
during the Indian Mutiny. However, as a
landowner he valued progress above
popularity. He increased rents to pay for
improvements to Rousay and evicted
tenants who spoke against him. He has
been described as 'the worst of the
19th-century lairds in Orkney'.

Walk left along the road for 500m to
reach a small parking bay just past the
sign to Taversoe Tuick Chambered Cairn.
Go through the gate and up the track.
Being this close to the only complete two-
storey cairn in Orkney, it would be a
shame not to look inside.

After exploring the cairn, carry on up
the track and keep to the right to go
through the gate onto the path by the
wall. Turn right at the top, to another gate
behind the cottage. This opens into a field
which can get very churned up by cattle

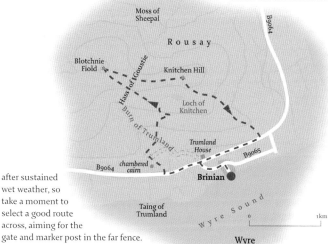

after sustained wet weather, so take a moment to select a good route across, aiming for the gate and marker post in the far fence.

Climb the stile by the gate and you have arrived at the RSPB Reserve. A marker post shows the way up the path. It leads through the heather to join another track with an option to go left or right. Go left in the direction of the 'Long Trail'. Follow the regular marker posts, soon forking left where the path splits, then bear right at another fork 230m further on. The marker posts lead you up the hillside, then direct you leftwards to the small cairn on the top of Blotchnie Field.

In summer, clear air can make for spectacular views southwards over Wyre and Gairsay to Kirkwall Bay, and over the North Isles in the other direction. Summer is also the best time to see birds such as red-throated diver, hen harrier, merlin and short-eared owl. There are bonxies here as well, so keep your wits about you lest you come under attack.

The next target is the summit of Knitchen Hill, 23m lower and just over 1km along the ridge to the east. There is no obvious path across the grass and heather but the marker posts are easy to follow, and the cairn on Knitchen Hill should be visible if you are unsure!

The path home is easy to follow, traversing the hillside at times but generally heading in the direction of the northern end of Wyre. It is joined by a path from the right at a telegraph pole (the route taken by those who opted for the 'Short Trail'), winding down through gorse bushes and around a garden fence before emerging onto the public road. Turn right, then left at the Trumland gates to return to the pier.

◀ Looking down from Trumland RSPB Reserve

Egilsay and St Magnus' Church

Distance **11.5km** Time **4 hours**
Terrain **deserted roads, farmland with
livestock, thick grass (and rocky
foreshore if you return by the coast)**
Map **OS Explorer 464** Access **regular
ferries from Tingwall to Egilsay**

**Visit the place where St Magnus was
murdered and a church was built in his
honour, before heading south across
farmland maintained by the RSPB as a
habitat for the corncrake, a shy bird with
a distinctive rasping call.**

St Magnus' Church, with its tall round
tower, dominates the island. To reach it
from the pier, walk up to a stile just
before the first farm on the left, then
follow the path along the field to the
heavy kirkyard gates.

After exploring the ruins and the
cemetery, take the track inland and turn
right at the road. Walk down to the
crossroads and turn left for the
old Egilsay school which closed
in 2011. Now leased by the local
community, it is a good place
to find shelter during your visit

if you need it. The door is never locked
and there are tea and coffee facilities
(with an honesty box), local books and
wi-fi connection.

Just beyond the school, a gate on the
right provides access to a cenotaph
marking the spot where Magnus
Erlendsson is thought to have been
executed on the orders of his cousin
Hakon, with whom he had shared the
Earldom of Orkney. As he had been a
popular and pious man, a cult grew up
around Magnus and a number of miracles
were soon attributed to him, eventually
leading to his canonisation in 1135. In 1919
a wooden box containing his remains was
found during renovation work in the
Cathedral that bears his name in Kirkwall.

Return to the crossroads and go left to
follow the public road south. Some 2km
further on, after a slight left and then a
right bend, you will finally come to
Onziebust Farm. Go through the
farmyard where you will be faced with a
line of three gates. Take the leftmost

gate and walk between the fences to the Hillocks of the Graand, where the remains of a chambered cairn provide a vantage point from which to survey the southern tip of the island. Walk on across the grass, heading left to a gate above the shore and turn right.

In summer, you need to be wary of young fulmars nestled into the banks. Disturb them at your peril! From here, you can walk along the shore, with dramatic upward slabs of rock, or battle your way through the dense grass round the Loch of the Graand.

Once round the southern tip, head up the west coast past the loch. If the tide is high, you might prefer to cut across the field to your right to pick up a track back to Onziebust Farm and retrace your steps to the ferry terminal. Otherwise walk along the rocks until you pass the cottage built close to the shore, opposite the Point of Vady.

After keeping a respectful distance from the cottage, climb onto the track and go uphill for about 300m to a gate on the left. This will allow you back down to the water's edge. Turn right to continue walking north along the shore, traversing

the field at the head of the inlet to follow the faint path outside the fence.

Cross the ladder stile when you come to it, then immediately climb the stile to your right and walk north in the wide grassy pasture between the two fences. This will bring you down past the house at Whistlebare and onto a track back to the public road by the ferry terminal.

Wyre and Cubbie Roo's Castle

Distance 7km **Time** 2 hours 30
Terrain quiet island road, farm track
through fields and coastal path
Map OS Explorer 464 **Access** ferry from
Tingwall to Wyre

**Best known as the childhood home of the
writer Edwin Muir and the site of Cubbie
Roo's Castle, Wyre makes for a lovely day
out. The Vikings called it Vigr – 'The
Spearhead' – and this walk goes right to
the sharp end. Take a picnic and explore
one of Orkney's smallest communities.**

Wyre has no shop so you will need to be
self-sufficient during your visit. Set off up
the road from the pier, turning right to
walk along the 'top' of the island. At its
highest, Wyre is just over 30m above sea
level and there is only 2.5km of public
road. You won't get lost!

The farm to your right as you head
down the island is The Bu. Poet and
novelist Edwin Muir spent his early
childhood here before increasing farm
rents forced his family to move to the
Orkney Mainland and then to Glasgow.
Muir would later describe the move as a
descent from the innocence of a rural
Eden into Hell, and the severe sense of
displacement never left him.

Shortly after the track to The Bu, you
will reach the Wyre Heritage Centre, a
good source of information about the
island and its history. Head down the
track by the centre to St Mary's Chapel, a
small church built towards the end of the
12th century.

From the western perimeter wall, over
the grandest stile in Orkney, is a short
path leading to Cubbie Roo's Castle, the

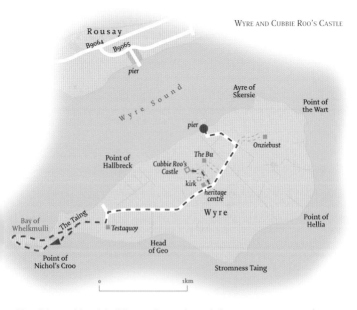

older of the two historic buildings and very possibly the oldest stone castle in Scotland. Built by a Viking called Kolbein Hrúga in the first half of the 12th century, it was a mighty square tower. It was also effective. The only time it came under siege the attack failed and the two sides eventually declared a truce. Cubbie Roo was a legendary Orcadian giant who made Wyre his home when he wasn't leaping between islands.

The chapel is thought to have been built either by Kolbein or his son Bjarni, the Bishop of Orkney. Continue the walk by retracing your steps past the chapel to the road and turning right to head in a southwesterly, then westerly direction. Where the road forks, go left. Follow

the track down past Testaquoy and out across the fields, opening and closing gates as required.

After the drystane dyke, the track bends left for the shore. You have arrived at The Taing; uncultivated, wet underfoot, and much loved by seals and birds. Follow the shoreline round the point, being careful not to disturb the arctic terns during their nesting season, and watching out for seals hauled out on the rocks at low tide.

There are a number of old walls and other structures to explore, such as a row of kelp pits (hard to find down near the point) and two mounds thought to be burial chambers. When it is time to go, return to the track past Testaquoy and follow the road back to the ferry slip.

◂ Old Tongaday, Wyre

Shapinsay and Balfour Castle

Distance 8km **Time** 3 hours
Terrain coastal paths, rocky shores and
quiet public roads **Map** OS Explorer 461
Access ferry from Kirkwall to Shapinsay

**The Balfour family certainly left its mark
on Shapinsay, remodelling the house,
village and harbour before setting out
uniform field boundaries which remain
in place today. Survey their handiwork
with this easy walk between ferries.**

Whatever their virtues, the Balfours
were clearly not troubled by modesty.
They transformed the family home, then
changed its name from Cliffdale to
Balfour Castle. After remodelling the
village of Shoreside, they renamed it
Balfour. When stepping ashore, look for
the little building tucked into the wall
near the top of the slipway. This was a
public toilet, flushed by the tides twice a
day and built – inevitably – by the
Balfours. The castle is now an exclusive
hotel and the grounds are private.

Walk towards the Gatehouse, the
flat-roofed building overlooking the
harbour, which used to straddle the main
drive to the castle. Facing the Gatehouse,
you'll see a gap to its immediate right.
This will allow you to walk along the
back of the building and through the
gate into the field. The round tower,
known as the Douche, was built as a
doocot (dovecot), but was later
converted into a saltwater shower.

As the path carries on across the pasture,
it allows good views of the castle. Go
through the gate in the drystane dyke by
the old pier, and follow the shoreline. To
your right is one of several artificial ponds
created to attract shooting parties. Go
round the southwestern headland, cross a
stile, and then you will be heading north.

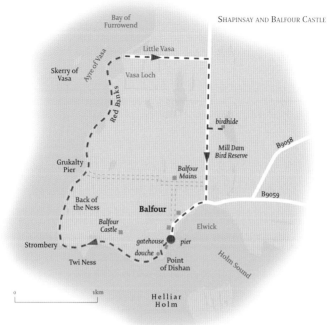

At the next dyke, drop down onto the shore and cross the old Grukalty Pier, a drystone construction which is effectively an extension of the dyke. From here, it is easier to walk along the shore because the grass above is thick and full of tussocks. You will pass the remains of a cast-iron millwheel lying among the stones before you reach the Red Banks, where coastal erosion is steadily eating into the land.

At the far end, the path reappears on the grassy strip between the shore and Vasa Loch. Keep to the shore to avoid disturbing the arctic terns in the spring and early summer. Beyond the loch, a track leads onto a public road before turning away from the shore, beside Little Vasa Water, and heading inland.

Follow the road for 1km to the junction at the top of the hill, then turn right. From here it is a straight walk back to the village. Leave time to visit the RSPB's Mill Dam Reserve which you pass on your left. The hide provides a wonderful view down over the old mill pond.

Turn right at the junction at the bottom of the hill. Seals like to haul themselves out of the water at low tide all along the shore here and they seem remarkably unflustered by human activity. The attractive row of cottages will lead you back to the pier.

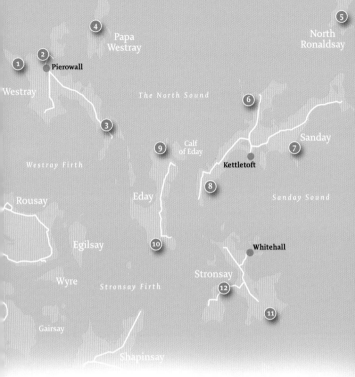

The map shows the following labelled locations:

- ① Westray
- ② Pierowall
- ③
- ④ Papa Westray
- ⑤ North Ronaldsay
- ⑥
- ⑦ Sanday
- ⑧
- ⑨ Calf of Eday
- ⑩
- ⑪
- ⑫ Stronsay

Kettletoft

Whitehall

The North Sound

Westray Firth

Rousay

Eday

Egilsay

Wyre

Stronsay Firth

Sanday Sound

Gairsay

Shapinsay

The Outer North Isles include Orkney's remotest communities of North Ronaldsay and Papa Westray, or Papay as it is known locally. With infrequent cargo ferries, these islands rely heavily on the inter-island air service from Kirkwall, operated by Loganair. They are all the more fascinating for the fragile connections to the outside world. While Westray, Sanday, Stronsay and Eday also enjoy daily flights, they have a regular ferry service from Kirkwall operated by Orkney Ferries.

Although they have much in common, the islands are markedly different. Mostly, you can rely on a beach to suit any wind direction, historic sites, seals, seabirds, wildflowers, breathtaking scenery and a friendly welcome. Together and separately they promise a rich experience for the visitor.

Stone of Setter ▶

The Outer North Isles

Noup Head

Distance **7km** Time **2 hours**
Terrain **coastal path and surfaced roads**
Map **OS Explorer 464** Access **ferry from Kirkwall to Rapness with connecting bus to Pierowall, 3km from the start**

A classic clifftop walk to Westray's western headland with stunning views, maritime heathland and a picturesque lighthouse.

Noup Head is well signposted from Pierowall village and the walk starts from a small parking area provided by the farmer at Backarass on the left-hand side of the road, just before the steading.

Head through the kissing gate below the car park and down the hillside between the fences, turning right after you have crossed the two stiles onto the coastal path. The cliffs here are comparatively low-lying, but they still produce an impressive natural arch which you can see if you glance back as you walk towards the next stile. This can be a wild place in winter but in summer the clifftops are carpeted in wildflowers; sea pinks and spring squill are everywhere.

The views to the south can be magnificent, with Rousay closest, the wedge-shaped profile of The Brough of Birsay further west and, on clear days, the northern coast of Scotland in the distance. Soon a stile and information board mark the beginning of the RSPB's Noup Cliffs Nature Reserve.

On the way to the lighthouse, there are several good (but high) vantage points from which you can see the sandstone

cliff faces, weathered into numerous horizontal ledges, which make perfect nesting places for the birds. The smell is pungent even on a windy day.

On the landward side of the path, beware arctic terns which can be easily disturbed during the breeding season. As the path gradually begins to climb, marker posts wisely suggest you keep back from the cliff edge.

The force of the sea has created many caves and stacks along this stretch of Westray's coast. Probably best known – although impossible to see without the help of a local guide – is the Gentlemen's Cave where four local lairds with Jacobite sympathies hid for several months after

backing the losing side in the rebellion of 1745. Easier to spot is the great fluted cliff face known as John Harcus' Windows.

The lighthouse sits on top of 50m-high cliffs and was built in 1898, inevitably by a member of the industrious Stevenson family. The lightkeepers' cottages were demolished after the light was automated in 1964.

From here, follow the lighthouse road inland with fine views over to the northern tip of Westray and Papa Westray beyond. You will pass close to the Loch of the Stack on your right (often used by seabirds to clean their plumage) and the ruined homestead of North House before joining the surfaced public road just after Noup Farm. From here, it is only a short way back uphill and along to the car park at **Backarass**.

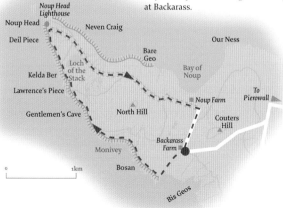

Noltland Castle and Grobust

Distance 6km **Time** 2 hours
Terrain minor roads and some rough
sandy paths **Map** OS Explorer 464
Access ferry from Kirkwall to Rapness,
with connecting bus to Pierowall;
passenger ferry from Papa Westray to
Gill Pier, around 1.3km from the start

**An easy walk from the village to explore a
medieval kirk, an Elizabethan castle and
an Iron Age broch, not forgetting one of
the finest sandy beaches in Westray.**

Westray's population may be fewer than
600, but the island appears to be thriving
both culturally and economically, with
Pierowall at its centre. The village has
grown up around the bay and boasts
shops, an hotel, a café, a gallery, post
office, church, bank, school and even a
part-time chip shop.

Park beside the cemetery at the 13th-
century Lady Kirk, 500m north of the
school. With the remains of the kirk
behind you, walk up between the fire
station and the Hofn Centre, turning left
at the top. After a few hundred metres,

take the second turn on your right and
walk up to a junction.

Turn right, then left, and follow the
road to Noltland Castle. You can tell from
the number of gun holes in the walls that
the builder of this place was expecting
trouble. Gilbert Balfour was involved in
the murder of Cardinal Beaton in 1546,
then two decades later he helped dispatch
Mary Queen of Scots' second husband,
Lord Darnley. When Mary was arrested
soon afterwards, Gilbert headed home to
Westray where the gun holes no doubt
gave him a sense of security.

Noltland was part-fortress, part-
residence, although it seems the castle was
never fully completed. The walk continues
up the road to the crossroads, where it

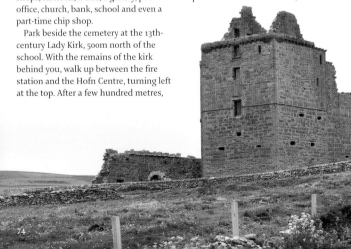

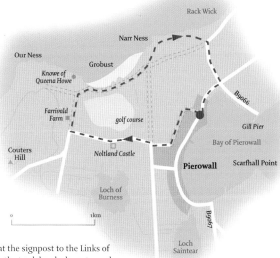

turns right at the signpost to the Links of Noltland. As the track heads down towards the shore, past Farrivald Farm, you will see the Knowe of Queena Howe over to your left, the remains of an Iron Age broch.

Go right, down to Grobust beach, between the low stone walls. These are 'tangle dykes' where seaweed stalks were dried before being sent away for processing, an industry which provided a useful source of income for generations of islanders until the 1980s.

The Links of Noltland, the extensive sandy area above the beach, is rich in archaeology. Close by, the rock which slopes down into the water midway along the beach is well known for fossilised fish set into its blue-grey slabs. Seals will probably follow your progress from the

sea as you head off the beach, past another series of tangle dykes, onto the network of paths which criss-cross the rough grassland.

Veer away from the shore at this point, aiming to join the minor road which runs parallel to the coast. Turn right along the road, heading back towards Pierowall Bay, turning right and right again in quick succession at two junctions. As you follow the road back round to the village, you will see Gill Pier over to your left. Ferries arrived here until the introduction of ro-ro in 1990, although it is still used by the local fishing fleet and the passenger ferry to Papa Westray.

◂ Noltland Castle

Castle o'Burrian and the Bay of Tafts

Distance 5.5km **Time** 2 hours
Terrain grassy paths, boggy in places,
farm tracks and minor roads
Map OS Explorer 464 **Access** ferry from
Kirkwall to Rapness, with connecting bus
– ask the driver to stop at the Castle
o'Burrian road end; or walk from the ferry
pier, joining the route at the junction off
the B9066 for the Bay of Tafts after 1km

If you want to see puffins, this is the
place to go. From April to August your
chances of spotting the birds at close
quarters are better here than anywhere
else in Orkney. This walk takes you from
the North Sea to the Atlantic with
derelict mills, dramatic cliffs and a sandy
beach along the way.

You cannot miss the turning to the
Castle o'Burrian off the B9066. It is 2km
north of the Rapness pier and is marked
by a colourful sign pointing to 'Puffins'.
Park at the old Rapness Mill and take the
footpath round the back of the building
along the top of the cliffs.

The Castle o'Burrian stack is just a few
minutes' walk along the cliffs and there is
plenty of space to settle down and watch
the hundreds of puffins which nest here
in the early part of the summer. You may
be able to make out the remains of a
building on the summit, said to be the
site of an early Christian hermitage.

There are likely to be more puffins on
the cliffs beyond the Castle and, if you are
lucky, you will see them sitting very close
to the path. While the puffins are the
headline act, you may also come across
shags, razorbill, fulmar and guillemot.

The path continues close to the edge of

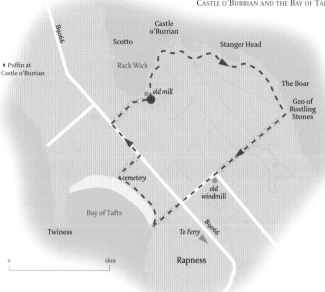

the cliffs with plenty of rock formations, wildflowers, such as sea campion and wild thyme, and seabirds adding interest until it opens out at Stanger Head. The cliffs on this impressive headland have fractured to create two windows in the rock face which the North Sea pours through when the swell is strong.

After Stanger Head, the path follows the fenceline and is quite boggy in places, although it is usually possible to find a dry route around the worst bits. After crossing the stile (by the Geo of Rustling Stones), turn right and go up the grass track. It gradually improves as it heads over the hill, joining a minor road

downhill. You will pass the old Stanger Mill, a wind-driven threshing mill with a round kiln used to dry the grain. The sails have gone, but the wooden pole and gearing remain.

Cross the B9066 onto the farm track leading towards the sea at the Bay of Tafts. Turn right at the bottom and drop onto the sand at the first opportunity to walk along the beach, keeping an eye out for wading birds along the water's edge. Halfway round the bay, take the sandy track which leads up past the graveyard to the main road. Turn left and, after 400m, turn right at the puffin sign to make your way back to the start.

Papa Westray

Distance 16km **Time** 5 hours 30
Terrain farm tracks, grassy paths and
quiet roads **Map** OS Explorer 464
Access regular flights from Kirkwall;
infrequent ferry from Kirkwall and
summer passenger ferry from Westray

Allow plenty of time to walk the entire
coastline of Papa Westray or take this
potted tour of the island's highlights.
Everything from Europe's oldest house
to the world's shortest scheduled flight
makes Papay, as it's known to locals, a
fascinating place to visit.

The flight from Westray is in the
Guinness Book of Records as the shortest
scheduled air route in the world and it is a
great way to arrive in Papay, but seats are
much in demand, so book your ticket well
in advance. If arriving by air, turn right
from the airstrip and follow the public
road down to Moclett Pier at the south
end of the island. This is where you step

ashore if you come by sea. From the pier,
take the grassy track on the right which
leads through a gate and round the
headland. Cross the exposed flagstones to
follow a narrow path winding north along
the coastline, keeping an eye out for
otters below the cliffs as you go.

Where the path joins a farm track beside
the shore, a gap in the stone dyke to your
left lets you cross the field to the ruins of
St Tredwell's Chapel. The medieval
building is on the site of a broch, which
itself was built on a crannog. Return to
the track and follow it north, eventually
leading inland to join the public road
down to the old Nouster pier.

Walk behind the old pier buildings and
drop down onto the sand to walk round
the South, then North Wicks. If the tide is
out, look for the tidal pool at Weelie's
Taing where there are some interesting
and unexplained archaeological remains.

The path continues northwards, past a

◀ The Knap of Howar

complex of planticrus (at least one of which is still in use) and along the short grass beside flagstone cliffs. A stile lets you cross the fence, and the path runs outside the dyke to the memorial at the spot where Orkney's last great auk was shot in 1813. The last in the British Isles was killed in 1840 when residents of St Kilda beat it to death, believing it was a witch responsible for a wild storm.

Climb the stile a few metres further on, then head back across the short grass with the dyke to your left, looking out for the rare *primula scotica* as you go. Cross the two stiles back onto the path and retrace your steps to the tidal pool. Turn right onto the public road and follow it uphill and round to the left, before walking south for just over 1km.

Beside the road is a traditional cottage with a flagstone roof where a sign points right to St Boniface Church, one of only two Orkney churches to survive the Reformation. After exploring the old kirk, take the turnstile by the gate and go down onto the rocks where the remains of a broch stick out of the bank, along with evidence of other ancient buildings and middens.

Follow the shoreline south to the remarkable Knap of Howar, a Neolithic farmstead and the oldest constructed stone house in Europe, preserved by

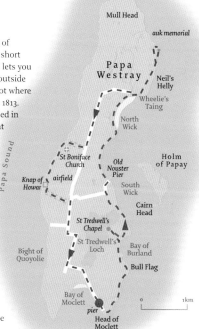

windblown sand. A path leads inland across the field to the track to Holland Farm, where the Bothy Museum is always open.

If you need refreshments, Beltane House, a community-run cooperative, is not far. The airstrip is a short way up the road to the north, but if you came by boat turn right and follow the road back to Moclett Pier.

North Ronaldsay

Distance 17.5km **Time** 5 hours 30
Terrain rocky coastal paths, grassland
and very quiet roads **Map** OS Explorer 465
Access Loganair operates daily flights
from Kirkwall Airport; seats are at a
premium so advance booking is essential

**North Ronaldsay amply repays those who
stay overnight but, for anyone on a
daytrip, this route is easily manageable
between flights and leads you round
much of the shoreline, with sheep,
seabirds and seals for company.**

The flight out from Kirkwall provides a
bird's-eye view of the North Isles and is a
joy in itself. Once on the ground, follow
the road round from the airstrip to the
war memorial where a right turn will take
you south. As you walk downhill – with
the pier in the distance – look for a
green footpath diagram marking
the start of a path to the right.

Follow it towards the sea, with an
impressive perforated monolith

called The Stan Stane in the field to your
right. Now you have your first view of the
sheep dyke, the stone wall which once
encircled the island to keep the seaweed-
eating sheep on the shore. As you turn
left to walk outside the dyke, you will
probably see sheep on the rocks below.
Bones of very similar animals have been
found at the Neolithic village of Skara
Brae, suggesting the breed has changed
little in 5000 years.

As you round the southern headland
(in fact, anywhere the path passes close
to the wall), watch for fulmars nesting at
the base of the dyke. They do not like to
be surprised!

From the jetty, walk along the road
for 250m, where you will pass the
entrance to the Bird Observatory.
It provides a useful café for passing
walkers. After a few paces, take the track
down to the beach on the right which
leads you to the Broch of Burrian on
North Ronaldsay's southernmost tip.

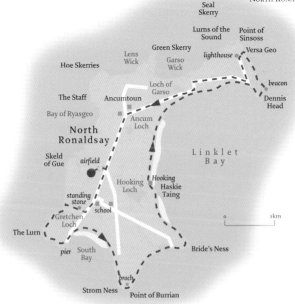

Seal
Skerry

Lurns of the
Sound

Point of
Sinsoss

Green Skerry

Versa Geo

lighthouse

Lens
Wick

Garso
Wick

Hoe Skerries

beacon

Loch of
Garso

Dennis
Head

The Staff

Ancumtoun

Bay of Ryasgeo

Ancum
Loch

North
Ronaldsay

Linklet
Bay

Skeld
of Gue

airfield

Hooking
Loch

Hooking
Haskie
Taing

standing
stone

school

0   1km

Gretchen
Loch

The Lurn

pier

South
Bay

Bride's Ness

Strom Ness

broch

Point of Burrian

A storm beach will take you to the next headland, called Bride's Ness, and soon to a set of *punds*, stone enclosures used for gathering and sorting the sheep. Walk on the beach below Hooking Farm, then up onto the wide flat links – also the island's golf course – which stretch for most of the length of Linklet Bay. The old coastguard lookout hut against the wall now serves as the clubhouse.

At the north end of the bay, keep to the rocks to avoid nesting arctic terns and follow the curve of the shore round to the old beacon on Dennis Head, with its large sandstone orb on the top. Again, the terns will let you know if you come too close.

Walk across the pasture by the row of planticrus to the 'new' lighthouse, where there are interpretation panels, a museum, workshop and a fine café/restaurant in the former lightkeeper's accommodation.

On a clear day you can see Fair Isle, the southernmost island of Shetland, 40km to the northeast – there's an even better view from the top of the lighthouse.

To head home, follow the road past the communications towers to the shore, where it turns sharp right. After a couple of obvious left turns, the road leads back to the war memorial, with the airstrip on your right.

Sanday and the Holms of Ire

Distance 10km (3km less if the tide is high) **Time** 3 hours **Terrain** mostly farm tracks with some slippery rocks to cross to the islands **Map** OS Explorer 465 **Access** ferry from Kirkwall to Sanday, with connecting bus which stops on request; booking must be made the day before

Take a turn round two tidal islands on the northwest corner of Sanday. Seals, seabirds, wrecks and ruins make this a delightful outing. Be warned that the Holms are tidal and become inaccessible on a rising tide. Always check tide times and seek local advice before crossing.

Dating from the 17th century, the house at Scar was once at the heart of a thriving estate, with its own forge, mill and schoolroom. Although somewhat dilapidated, it makes a good starting point with plenty of parking at the nearby kirkyard. To find it, head north from the ferry terminal and turn left after 10km where it is signposted to Burness.

Scar is at the very end of the B9068. With the kirkyard on your left, and the round base of an old windmill in the field to your right, head along to the information board where a left turn will take you down the track towards Scar. The house is privately owned and the outbuildings are part of a working farm, so stay on the track as it leads through the steading, keeping the corrugated green shed on your left.

Bear left along the line of sheds and follow the track as it bends right, round to the old mill at Woo and on between the stone dykes heading west. Continue to go straight, between fences, then along the side of the fields, opening and closing gates where necessary, until you reach the shore close to an impressive cairn.

Turn left along the ayre which separates Roos Loch from the sea, keeping an eye out for signs of otters which can be found here. At the road, turn right and follow it up onto open ground, heading for the cairn on the brow of the hill. With the

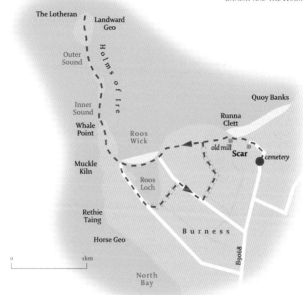

northern cliffs of Eday in the distance, you get a fine view over the Holms.

Whether you can go further depends on the tides – only cross on an ebbing tide or your visit could be longer than intended. There are several small buildings on the Inner Holm, including an ancient chapel – although little remains of it – and a row of well-preserved planticrus (shelters used to grow seedlings). At low tide, you might see the wreckage of the *Alex Hastie*, a trawler which ran aground in 1940 on the furthest point of the Outer Holm. Nothing remains, however, of the Dutch frigate *Utrecht* which sank here in 1807 with the loss of around 100 lives.

Once back across the tidal sound, follow the road inland until you near the end of Roos Loch, where a grassy track on the left leads between fields to reach another public road. Turn right, then left after 450m, just after a small house with derelict outbuildings. When this track turns right towards the farm, continue straight on to the corner of the field, ignoring the gate and bending left to walk with the field dyke at your right hand. This will bring you back to familiar territory. Turn right where it meets the farm track flanked by drystane dykes, and follow the track back past Scar to the kirkyard.

◀ The cemetery at Scar

Tresness

Distance 9.5km **Time** 2 to 3 hours
Terrain sandy beaches and grassy tracks,
wet in places **Map** OS Explorer 465
Access ferry from Kirkwall to Sanday, with
connecting bus which stops on request;
booking must be made the day before

**Explore Orkney's most impressive stretch
of sand dunes on the way to Sanday's
quiet Tresness peninsula. Interesting
whenever you go, but best at low tide.**

There is a grassy parking area 1.5km east
of Lady Village just off the B9069. The
entrance is soon after the wartime
building beside the road. Known locally
as the Brickie Hut, it was part of a decoy
airfield built during the Second World War
to distract enemy planes from Scapa Flow.

The route to Tresness begins as a grassy
track above Cata Sand, a shallow inlet
transformed by the tide; a sea loch at high
water but wide sandflats when the tide is
out. It is easy and safe to take a shortcut
at low tide if your footwear is waterproof!

There are often tyre tracks across the
sand as vehicles come and go from
Tresness Farm. To your left is a high bank
of sand dunes, stabilised by marram
grass, which encloses Cata Sand. Where
the sand is less stable at the southern tip,
there is a large dune which has been
separated from the rest. To your right is
the mouth of Cata Sand, known as the
Clogg, which appears narrow from the top
of the dune, but the water is deep and
treacherous. Do not be tempted to use it
as a shortcut home.

Walk across onto Tresness and keep left
where the track forks. The farmhouse has

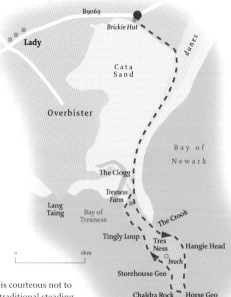

been restored, so it is courteous not to pass too close. The traditional steading can be admired from the path with its unusual hexagonal 'horse gang' – where horses walked round and round to drive a threshing mill next door.

From the buildings, follow the track towards the south end of the peninsula, passing an area of wetland on the way. Just beyond the trig point, at the southernmost tip of Tresness, is a chambered cairn clinging to the edge of the low cliff. With much exposed stonework it is fun to visit, but it is a popular nesting place for fulmars who may make you regret your curiosity if you take them by surprise!

The easiest way home from here is simply to retrace your steps. Alternatively, you can return via the west coast of Tresness by continuing round the headland, walking between the field boundaries and the sea. It is a slightly shorter route home, but hard going in places with no discernible path to follow through the grassy tussocks. This route makes it easy to visit the Broch of Wasso, on your right, before crossing back onto the dunes and – if the tide is out – trying to count the lugworm casts on Cata Sand as you make your way home.

Doun Helzie

Distance 6km **Time** 2 hours
Terrain farm tracks and grassy paths with
patches of nettles; no access to cliffs and
caves at high tide **Map** OS Explorer 465
Access ferry from Kirkwall to Sanday, with
connecting bus – ask the driver to stop at
the Stove junction, 900m from the start;
booking must be made the day before

**This little gem (pronounced 'Doun
Hellie') lies only a short walk over the
brow of a hill, but at low tide is one of the
most magical beaches in Orkney. It
boasts steep dunes and virgin sand with
spectacular caves and cliffs. Bring a torch.**

From the ferry terminal, follow the
B9070 uphill for almost 4km to the sharp
right-hand bend. After another 400m, turn
right down the minor road (signposted to
Stove, but only from the other direction!)
and park by the electricity substation.

Walk back up the road for about 300m,
turning right onto a sandy farm track.
This heads to a gate at the top of the field.
Although this gate is often open, do not
go through it, but take the path on your

right and follow it down between the
dyke and the fence. At the corner, bear left
and walk down the slope towards the sea.

As soon as the fence allows, turn left
along a narrow, rough path to the top of
the dunes. The quickest way – probably
the most fun as well – is to charge
headlong down the dunes onto the beach
below. If you want to descend more
gently, walk to the far end where access to
the beach is easy.

To explore the cliffs, turn to your right
and head south, past the redundant
electricity cable suspended between the
beach and the dunes. Seabirds will
probably follow you until they decide you
are no longer of interest. Soon you will
find a rock passage, complete with a
window allowing a delightful view back
along the beach. Some of the caves are
quite deep and a torch makes it easier to
appreciate the beauty of the rocks. Be
prepared for the odd fright if you disturb
a pigeon nesting within! As the cave
floors are swept clean with every high
tide, yours will probably be the only
footprints. Do not get caught out by the
tide as you explore the succession of little
beaches between the bluffs. You won't be

▼ Doun Helzie beach

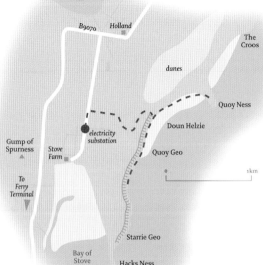

stranded (unless you fall asleep), but you might have to walk home with wet feet.

Once you have fully explored the caves and cliffs, it is time to enjoy the beach. There are many different shells to be found in Sanday and Doun Helzie is a great place to look for them, particularly along the high water mark. Look out, too, for otter tracks. Otters are not unknown around here and their distinctive footprints – five toes arching round the front of a large pad – show up well in the sand. If you spot any tracks, you might be lucky enough to see the otter that made them.

At the north end of the beach is Quoy Ness, the low-lying headland beyond which there may be common and grey seals hauled out on the rocks. From here, walk back along the dunes and up onto the path to the start.

Eday Heritage Walk

Distance 10km **Time** 3 hours 30
Terrain well-trodden paths, heather
moorland and minor roads
Map OS Explorer 465 **Access** ferry from
Kirkwall, Stronsay and Sanday to Eday;
bus connects with morning and evening
ferries on Thursdays only from May to
September; it will drop off and pick up at
the Eday shop if requested

**A wonderful yomp round the north end
of Eday with outstanding views, tales of
piracy, an unusual lighthouse and, as you
can guess from the title, no shortage of
ancient monuments.**

Eday's community shop, 8km north of
the ferry terminal, makes a good start
point with plenty of parking close by.
Set off towards the Mill Loch, past the bird
hide and through the kissing gate onto the
path leading up to the iconic 4.5m-high
Stone of Setter. Lichen-covered, weathered
and tapered, it resembles a giant hand and
is one of Orkney's tallest monoliths.

A boardwalk leads you on in the
direction of a stone shed – a former
school – under the hill to your left. Its
eastern gable points towards the Bronze
Age Fold of Setter, a wide circular stone
and turf embankment – purpose
unknown – just discernible in the grass
this side of the fence. Continue to the
next marker post by the remains of a
stalled burial cairn, its upright slabs
protruding through the turf.

The path leads over another boardwalk
to the two-storey Huntersquoy Tomb,
although only the ground floor remains.
It is uphill from here to Vinquoy Cairn,
impressively restored and accessible
through a small gate. Ignore the marker
post pointing to Cusbay Circular Walk and
head northwards across the heather,
making for the squat cairn on the summit
of Vinquoy Hill.

The view across the Calf of Eday and to
the other islands is superb, and the cairn
is a delightfully homespun island

identification aid – although you might find a map more useful.

Head onwards to the drystane dyke, turning right to drop down to a gate by the top of the woods. With the lighthouse in Carrick Sound over to your right, head along the hillside, maintaining height, to reach another dyke blocking your way. A tumbledown section by the corner to your right will let you across.

Follow the wall by your right hand round the corner until you can turn left. Where the track forks, go right, above the sheepfold and onto the hillside beyond. This path leads across the heather all the way to the trig point above the Red Head. Turn left and walk along the clifftops on the west side of Noup Hill with the peat banks for which the island is famous on your left.

When you reach a gate with a sign to Cusbay (which you should ignore), turn left and follow the fence, then the wall and finally just the path until you reach the lighthouse. From here, you can pick up the path that leads along the shore to Carrick House.

This was the house that the infamous Orkney Pirate, John Gow, was on his way to plunder when his ship ran aground on the Calf of Eday in 1724. After leading a murderous mutiny and raiding several ships in the Bay of Biscay, the local-boy-gone-bad's buccaneering career ended here: he was soon captured by his childhood schoolmate and owner of Carrick House, James Fea, and carted off to be hanged nine months later at Execution Dock in London.

Skirt round the back of the house to a wooden gate. Turn right onto the road up to Carrick Farm. Turn left by the steading, then right at the junction to follow the road back to the community shop.

◀ On Vinquoy Hill

Eday and the Point of Warness

Distance 5km **Time** 2 hours
Terrain coastal path, pasture and
moorland **Map** OS Explorer 465
Access ferries linking Eday with Kirkwall,
Stronsay and Sanday land at the pier
2.5km from the start of the walk

**Eday sits in the centre of Orkney's North
Isles and this walk climbs to its highest
point, giving unsurpassed views of the
surrounding islands.**

The start of the walk is 2.5km from the
ferry terminal. Take the first left as you
head up from the pier, then right, left and
right again at successive T-junctions.
There is a small parking area at the side of
the Greentoft farm road, and a stile in the
fence by the information board.

Heading right, the path leads you above
the shore. As you go round the first little
headland you are crossing the site of an
ancient chapel, known as Hannah's Kirk,
although coastal erosion has destroyed all
evidence of it. A few paces further takes
you across the overflow from the Lady
Well, a spring which rises beneath the
small building 250m inland.

Still on the path, follow the shoreline
down to the Point of Warness, the
southernmost tip of the island with views
to Stronsay over to your left, Shapinsay in
front, and Egilsay, with Rousay behind, to
your right. Nearest you are the Green
Holms, Muckle and Little, where hundreds
of seal pups are born each year, making it
an internationally important breeding
colony. There may also be seals – most
likely common – hauled up on the rocks
below Warness Point if the tide is out.
A quick (but not infallible) way to tell the

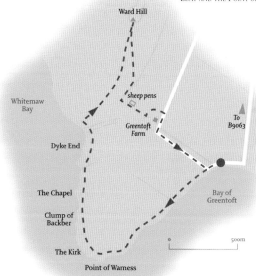

difference between common and grey seals is that common seals tend to lift their heads and tails when they are hauled up on dry land.

The walk now heads up the west side of Eday by crossing a stile and following the faint path above the cliffs. Offshore is a stretch of water called The Falls of Warness where the fast-flowing tides are ideal for testing tidal energy generators.

A gradual climb takes you towards Dyke End, a wide geo with south-facing cliffs. Cross the stile in the fence beside you (or take the gate further along) and set off across the pasture, making for the concrete building on the hill. There you will find a couple of posts which give directions to walkers and provide

somewhere for livestock to scratch.

Although the view is fine from here, it is even better 400m further on where a cairn and trig point mark the summit of Ward Hill. At 101m above sea level it is the highest point on the island. When you are ready, head back down, past the sheepfold and through the gate into the farmyard at Greentoft. Take care to avoid any farm machinery and livestock as you bear left between the buildings, then go right to join the track down to the shore.

As you head downhill towards your car, degraded ruins by the house at the edge of Greentoft Bay, slightly to your left, mark the site of the Castle of Stackel Brae, once a Norse stronghold, now being claimed by the sea at every winter storm.

◄ Eday shoreline

The Vat of Kirbister and Houseby

Distance 10.5km **Time** 4 hours
Terrain clifftop paths and country roads
Map OS Explorer 465 **Access** no public
transport to the start

**This corner of Stronsay boasts a
spectacular natural arch as well as
countless stacks, geos and broughs.
To say nothing of an Iron Age stronghold
which invites you to believe you are the
first to discover it!**

To reach the car park for The Vat of
Kirbister, head south from the ferry
terminal, turning left onto the B9060.
After 4.6km, turn left at the fire station
and follow the unmarked road, taking
the second road on your left. Take the
next right and park in the lay-by at
the signpost.

Head down the path towards the sea,
turning right along the cliffs and arriving,
after only a few minutes, at the Vat itself.

This was once a huge cave until the roof
collapsed, leaving only the narrow arch
spanning the entrance. The path
continues over a ditch and past a number
of small geos until it reaches a drystane
dyke. To your left are two rock stacks, the
southernmost of which is known as
Tam's Castle, with the remains of what is
believed to be a medieval hermitage
clearly visible on the grassy top.

The east coast of Stronsay has been
shaped by the sea into an intricate series
of geos and stacks, and the path winds its
way past them. In summer the narrow
ledges on the cliff faces are packed with
seabirds and there are bonxies and ravens
ready to harry them in search of food.
The wide heath between the cliffs and
the fields is alive with the call of curlew,
oystercatcher and greylag geese.

At Burgh Head, the path changes
direction, soon passing another ancient

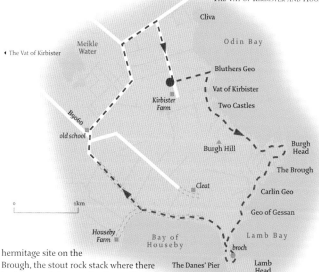

◀ The Vat of Kirbister

hermitage site on the Brough, the stout rock stack where there is also a good chance of seeing puffin in early summer.

Carry on along the cliff path, with the island of Auskerry to the south, round a couple of deep geos, over a stile and downhill to a rocky shore. The distinctive mound which dominates the narrow access to Lamb Head is worth investigating. There is not much left of the broch, but the two underground chambers which remain are accessible through holes in the roof, making them exciting to explore. The chambers once stood on either side of the entrance to the broch.

The route home begins by crossing the stile in the fence on the opposite side of the promontory. This is close to a natural spit, visible when the tide is out and

known as The Danes' Pier, suggesting it once served as a landing place for the Vikings.

Turn right along the track above the Bay of Houseby (also known as Housby and Housebay). At the concrete farm track (with a grass strip up the middle) turn right and walk inland. The track joins the surfaced road and bends right, leading you up past an old school building – keep to the right of the school – where it swings right again. Walk straight on for 1km, following the road as it curves left at Roadside Cottage. Go right at the T-junction and right again for the final leg, downhill and up again, to reach the start.

Rothiesholm

Distance 6km **Time** 2 hours
Terrain sandy beach, rough grassy paths
and one (often muddy) field
Map OS Explorer 465 **Access** no public
transport to the start

**A straightforward walk, if very boggy
at one point, along two contrasting
shorelines – sand and stones – with
birds and wildflowers in abundance.**

The first hurdle on this walk is in the
title: Rothiesholm is pronounced 'Rouse-
um'. The second lies on the crossing
between the shorelines where the ground
can be very wet and heavily trampled by
livestock. This requires careful
assessment of the best route on a good
day, and wellington boots on a poor one!

To reach the starting point, go south
from Whitehall for 4km until you see a

sign to Rothiesholm just before the fire
station. Turn right and drive for a further
2km, turning left where directed to
Rothiesholm Beach. Set off on foot over
the dunes and onto the sands.

This beach is well known as a good
spot for shell-seekers, and is the only
place in Orkney where the rare canoe
shell has been found so far. About 100m
short of the cottage at the far end, leave
the sand and look for the stile in the
fence by the road. Turn left, then right
through the kissing gate just beyond the
cottage. The path, now pretty rough,
heads inland with a deep ditch and fence
to your left and the Loch of Rothiesholm
to your right.

As it continues, the path leads through
thick grass, over a couple of boardwalks
and across a farm track. Where the fence

Index

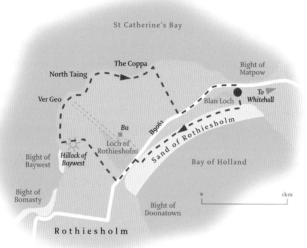

Rothiesholm

ends, head left across a grassy bridge towards the large mound in the middle of the field. This is a 3000-year-old burial chamber called the Hillock of Baywest and is on the most direct route to the shore on the far side. However, the ground beyond the hillock can be a quagmire and close to impassable. You might want to check from the summit, but the driest route is probably found by returning towards the grassy bridge, then following the fenceline to your left. Whichever way you go, aim for the stile in the fence beyond the far boardwalk.

The beach on this north-facing shore is very different, with the boulders rounded by the action of waves over centuries. A farm track running right makes the going easy to start with, but the path disappears when the track turns inland. Keep outside the fence in the tussocked grass above the shore – it soon gets easier! You may have to climb over a dilapidated gate at one point, but follow the shoreline until a modern fence with concrete posts prevents you going further. Turn inland to walk between the fences, over the brow and back to the road.

Turn left along the road. Ahead is the Blan Loch. Much loved by birds in winter, it is little more than a damp patch of ground in summer when, however, it comes alive with wildflowers such as marsh orchids and grass-of-parnassus. A right turn at the sign for Rothiesholm Beach reunites you with your car.